For a complete list of Management Books 2000 titles
visit our web-site on http://www.mb2000.com

FACETS OF LEADERSHIP

*Turning 'management thinking'
into 'management action'*

Selected readings from some of the world's gurus

**Dr Fred Cannon
Director, OED Consulting Ltd**

First published in 2009 by Management Books 2000 Ltd
Forge House, Limes Road
Kemble, Cirencester
Gloucestershire, GL7 6AD, UK
Tel: 0044 (0) 1285 771441
Fax: 0044 (0) 1285 771055
Email: info@mb2000.com
Web: www.mb2000.com

British Library Cataloguing in Publication Data is available

ISBN 9781852525927

Dedication

This book celebrates 10 years of management education, coaching and consulting provided by OED Consulting Ltd.

In addition to working some very enjoyable and often challenging clients I would like to thank three people who have worked with me during this time:

Catherine Purcell
Laura Tovey
Phil Lowe

For information about OED Consulting please contact:

Dr Fred Cannon, Director
Office: +44 (0) 1277 262 884
Direct: 0774 092 6701
Email: fredcannon@oedconsulting.com

Catherine Purcell, Research and Administration
Direct: 0797 1407717
Email: catherine.purcell@oedconsulting.com

Website: www.oedconsulting.com

Contents

Dedication   **5**

Introduction   **11**

1 Following the Hawks   **13**

2 Perspectives on Leadership   **22**

Reading 1. One more time – leadership and management – are they the same or different?
Dr Mike Young & Professor Vic Dulewicz   **30**

Reading 2. Two contrasting views of leadership
Professor Henry Minzberg & Frank Brown   **34**

Reading 3. Why should anyone be led by you?
Rob Goffee and Gareth Jones   **39**

Reading 4. Enabling bold visions
Jay A Conger & Douglas A Ready   **45**

Reading 5. Organisational climate and leadership styles
Daniel Goleman (in part)   **50**

Reading 6. Leading business performance
Dr Fred Cannon   **54**

Reading 7. The neuroscience of leadership
Kaizen Training   **59**

Reading 8. Are you a listening company?
Sunday Times Survey   **64**

3 Leading and Managing Performance   **67**

Reading 9. The high performance organisation
Harvard Business Review Collection   **72**

Reading 10. Leading extraordinary performance
Kim Cameron & Marc Lavine   **78**

Reading 11. The seven keys to high performance
Corporate Leadership Council   **81**

Reading 12. The seven deadly sins of performance management
Michael Hammer   **86**

Reading 13. Managing for high performance
Mckinsey Research   **91**

Reading 14. Coaching with edge: thoughts from a business coach
Dr Fred Cannon   **94**

Reading 15. The three signs of a miserable job
Patrick Lencioni   **101**

Reading 16. Creating Meaning at work
Roffey Park (Penna)   **105**

4   **Making the Team Work**   **110**

Reading 17. Teams at the Top
McKinsey Research   **118**

Reading 18. Senior leadership teams – what it takes to make them great
Ruth Wageman, Debra A. Nunes, James A. Burruss & J. Richard Hackman   **123**

Reading 19. Improving the performance of top teams
Andrew J. Ward et al   **129**

Reading 20. Engaging leadership in high performance teams
Professor Alimo-Metcalfe & Margaret Bradley   **133**

Reading 21. The five dysfunctions of a team
Patrick Lencioni   **136**

Reading 22. Making virtual teams work
John Symons & Claudia Stenzel   **142**

Reading 23. Big teams
Lynda Gratton & Tamara Erickson   **147**

5 Creating the future   **152**

Reading 24. Creating a climate for creativity and innovation
Goran Eckvall   **156**

Reading 25. How to become a management innovator
Gary Hamel   **162**

Reading 26. Breakthrough thinking from inside the box
Kevin P. Coyne, Patricia Gorman Clifford & Renee Dye **167**

Reading 27. Leadership for innovation
Joanna Barsh, Marla M. Capozzi & Jonathan Davidson) **172**

Reading 28. The role of corporate culture in radical innovation
Gerard J. Tellis, Jaideep C. Prabhu and Rajesh K. Chandy **176**

6 Making Things Happen   **180**

Reading 29. Making it happen
John Harvey-Jones   **183**

Reading 30. The secrets of getting people to say 'yes'
Robert B. Cialdini   **189**

Reading 31. Doing what's obvious but not easy
David Maister   **195**

Reading 32. Execution: the discipline of getting things done
Larry Bossidy & Ram Charan   **200**

Reading 33. Getting control of your life
David Allen   **205**

Reading 34. Business Behaving Badly
CHA   **209**

7 Postscript: *Reading 35.* The Best of Peter Drucker
Dr Fred Cannon   **216**

8 Reflective Summary   **228**

9 Home Truths   **231**

Tools 235

Appendix I. Effective Organisational Leadership (EOL) 236

Appendix II. Leader Behaviours 239

Appendix III. Performance Improvement Grid (PIG) 243

Introduction

In September 2005, OED Consulting began distributing a series of free 'management research updates' to its clients and professional contacts. The idea behind the MRU was born out of a sense of frustration felt by many practitioners about the difficulty involved in accessing 'ready-to-use' research.

What people told us was that either the research was not practically relevant or if it were it was often in a form which required very hard work to distil useable output. Put simply, research papers that have to meet strict publication criteria for respectable academic journals do not by nature lend themselves to easy bedtime reading.

At the other end of the spectrum, management abstracts, while useful in summarising the academic content of published articles, are not generally in a form that allows the practising manager to run with the idea. Our MRU's were designed to fill the gap: to help busy managers and professionals 'turn management thinking into management action'.

Each MRU comprises a brief summary of a contribution from the world of management research and writing. It may be an idea derived from a leading academic, a new book or a succinct summary of something worthwhile in one of the management journals. Whatever, it will have passed the test of usefulness and hopefully will be an easy read.

One of the familiar selling points of some of the leading business schools is the quality of their research and the fact that this can be incorporated into the schools' programmes for the benefit of its students. In a number of cases this is true. Talented members of faculty are able to convert their research into easy-to-understand deliverables. But it takes a very special kind of educator to be able to craft a paper that meets the criteria for a five-star journal and be able to teach it in a way that is meaningful to its executive students. Try thumbing through back copies of any five-star journal and see if you can find something that is immediately relevant to your world.

The 'readings' in this book are based primarily on adapted excerpts from the original materials. Every effort has been made to seek permissions from the authors and/or publishers of the original materials and acknowledgements are duly made where these have been requested. I hope you will find them not only useful in practical terms, but also enjoyable as a collection of thoughts by those who work in the world of management research and writing.

For ease of use, the 'readings' are grouped into five themes, which we refer to as *facets of leadership*. Each is preceded by a brief 'thought-piece'. We believe that mastery of these five 'facets' will prepare executives to make the quality of decisions that will be required to address the challenges that organisations face now and in the future.

1

Following the Hawks

The fulcrum of organisational change and survival is the point at which the external environment meets the organisational boundary. It is at this point that senior leaders – who we might refer to as 'big L' leaders – make decisions that can make or break the business. Many examples exist of companies that have not managed this interface as well as they might. Typical examples might include Ford, Jaguar and Marks & Spencer.

Effective organisational decisions are required in three broad areas: Strategy, Culture and Organisation Structure, Systems and Processes. Together, these form the organisational context within which leaders – whom we might refer to as 'little l' leaders – work at different levels in the organisation. Everything else is either a sub-set of, or related to, these three domains.

For 'big L' leaders to make effective decisions it goes without saying that they need to be able to identify, understand and capitalise on those trends that matter for their businesses – what John Varley, CEO of Barclays calls 'air currents'. Riding the 'air currents' – like paragliders who follow the hawks – helps to make success appear effortless. But the effort lies in finding those currents, in spotting the key trends in time or at least not losing sight of the ones the business is already riding. For Varley it was more privatisation of welfare, more wealth management, more demand for banking products in emerging markets, more credit card use and more demand from corporate customers for American-style debt-raising through the capital markets. With these in mind, the key challenge became one of building an organisation capable of responding effectively.

Most business executives around the world agree that global social, environmental and business trends are generally more important to corporate strategy than they were a few years ago. Equally important is the need for companies to act on these trends – to make effective organisational decisions across the three domains highlighted above. But first we need to agree what the common trends are facing companies now and in the years ahead.

We can get a helpful picture of the trends that businesses are facing by examining the various global surveys undertaken by McKinsey and others:

The researchers identify ten trends that they believe will transform the corporate landscape in the years ahead. These trends can be categorised into:

- three *macroeconomic trends* that will deeply transform the underlying global economy
- four *social and environmental trends* that could fundamentally change how we live and work
- three *business and industry trends* that will drive change at company level.

Macroeconomic Trends

1 Centres of economic activity will shift profoundly – not just globally but also regionally

The world has embarked on a massive realignment of economic activity. This realignment will persist. Within the next 20 years, the share of world GDP held by Western Europe and Asia will converge. For some industries and functions, the shift will be even more dramatic. The US will probably still account for the largest share of absolute economic growth.

2 *Public-sector activities will balloon making productivity gains essential*

The inexorable ageing of populations across the developed world will call for new levels of efficiency and creativity from the public sector. Without clear productivity gains the pension and health care burden will simply drive taxes to unprecedented levels. The management challenge is huge. The adoption of private-sector approaches will become pervasive.

3 *The consumer landscape will change and expand significantly*

Economic growth will push a billion new consumers into the global market place as household income crosses the critical threshold ($5,000) beyond which people begin to spend on discretionary goods. Shifts within consumer segments will also be profound and consumers, wherever they live, will increasingly have information about and access to the same products and brands.

Social and environmental trends

4 *Technological developments will transform the way people live and interact*

We are still in the early stages of the technology revolution. New developments are moving well beyond the realm of products and services. But more transformational than technology itself is the shift in behaviour that it enables. We work not just globally but instantaneously. We form and sustain relationships in new ways (12% of US newlyweds met online in 2006; two billion people use cell phones; a billion Google searches are activated daily with more than half in languages other than English). Geography is no longer the primary constraint on the limits of social and economic organisation.

15

5 *The battlefield for talent will shift*

The shift to knowledge-intensive industries highlights the importance and scarcity of well-trained talent. Vast new sources of talent are being opened up as a result of the integration of global labour markets. The 33 million university-educated young professionals in developing countries is more than double the number in developed ones. Global labour and talent strategies will be as important as sourcing and manufacturing strategies.

6 *The role and behaviour of big business will be more sharply scrutinised*

As business continue to expand their global reach, societal suspicion is likely to increase (think Tesco). Accepted tenets of global business ideology will be challenged (e.g. shareholder value, free trade, intellectual property rights etc.). Scandals and environmental mishaps (think BP) will exacerbate the situation thus fuelling resentment and creating political backlash. In short, big business will never be loved. Communication skills will be a critical competence of business leaders to ensure that the role of business and its contribution to society is well presented, understood and appreciated.

7 *Demand for natural resources will grow as will the strain on the environment*

We are using natural resources at unprecedented rates (e.g. oil demand is projected to grow by 50%). The world's resources are increasingly constrained. One of our scarcest resources – the atmosphere – will require dramatic shifts in behaviour. Opportunities for innovation – both technological and otherwise – flow from this.

16

Business and Industry Trends

8 New global industry structures are emerging

Non-traditional business models are flourishing, often co-existing in the same market sector. A flourish of smaller, fast-moving players will continue to emerge. Corporate borders are becoming more blurred as inter-linked ecosystems emerge. Robust private equity financing is changing corporate ownership. Winning companies will capitalise on these transformations.

9 Management will go from art to science

Bigger, more complex companies demand new tools to help leaders to run and manage them. Mega-institutions will become more viable. 'Gut instinct' management style will be less prevalent. Business leaders will become more scientifically trained to run their organisations. Scientific management will give companies the right to play the game.

10 Ubiquitous access to information is changing the economics of knowledge

Access to specialised knowledge has become almost universal and instantaneous. New models of knowledge production, access, distribution and ownership are emerging. Knowledge production is growing (e.g. worldwide patent applications rose from 1990 to 2004 at a rate of 20%). Companies will either need to learn how to leverage this new knowledge or risk drowning in information overload.

Six of these trends were considered of particular importance with 77% of the respondents citing growing numbers of consumers in emerging markets as important or very important to global business. The shift of economic activity between and within regions and the increasingly global nature of labour and talent markets also remain in the top group of trends, along with the increasingly availability of knowledge and a faster pace of technological innovation. All these were rated as important by over 70% of the respondents. In addition, one newcomer appeared in the top list – increasing constraints on the supply or usage of natural resources.

Leadership Challenges

These trends will present challenges for organisational leaders. First, the *assumptions* on which many businesses operate will be questioned. Those who fail to detect that the competitive landscape is changing, and changing fast, will be left behind. Secondly, organisations will need to *move quickly* in terms of decision-making, learning how to deal with both geographic and regional diversity (note the teething troubles experienced by Tesco in developing its US operations). Thirdly, they will have to make a quantum leap in their *ability* to execute, to get things done.

Identifying the trends is one thing, but acting to deal with them is another. A wide difference exists between assigning importance to trends and taking active steps to address them. Two-thirds of executives surveyed said that their organisations did not have a clear view of the changes needed to meet the looming economic and social developments although they readily agreed that organisational change was critical. Significantly, more than a third of executives believed that to meet the challenges that organisations face, it will be necessary to tackle a full range of 'hard' and 'soft' issues although confusion about how exactly to manage these issues was apparent.

If the mismatch between potential impact on profits and action is to be addressed, execution will need to become sharper. Whether organisations possess these skills internally is open to debate. Most companies looking for people to lead the changes expected them to be hired externally. In other words, deep-rooted change requires leadership and skills probably not found inside most organisations.

2008 Credit Crunch

Interestingly, as far as one can tell, nowhere among this or other survey data was the 2008 'credit crunch' predicted, itself a peculiar manifestation of the globalisation of markets and technological connectivity. People did not see it coming – or at least the executives who participated in the McKinsey and other surveys did not. Therein lies a lesson.

In his book, *When Markets Collide*, Mohamed El-Erian identifies the origins of the crisis in another miss-match – the ability of the financial system to undertake activities at a greater rate than could be sustained by the underlying infrastructure. When coupled with turbo-charged innovations it was inevitable that market accidents would occur. And they did – big time.

The point being made here, however, is not so much that executives across the world failed to predict the crisis, but that significant new trends were already changing the nature of global markets before the crisis. The rise of the emerging markets and the power of sovereign wealth funds were trends already firmly embedded before the credit crunch. In other words, it was not the failure to identify the trend but more a failure to identify – or recognise – the possible consequences of the trend.

Nevertheless, the crisis has made some trends of its own. Institutions are disappearing. The balance between market forces and the role of government is changing. The willingness of society to have a system that privatises massive gains and then socialises massive losses is losing favour, rapidly. The balance of influence shows signs of changing with America less at the financial epic-centre than hitherto. Most importantly, the global trends identified above cry out for global solutions that will not materialise to the extent they might unless trust across nations is restored. Strategic institutions such as the IMF have failed to keep up with the changing financial world. Another example of a miss-match. As Drucker states in his *Theory of the Business*: "The root cause of nearly every crisis is that the assumptions on which the organisation has been built no longer fit reality."

Little 'l' Leaders

But this is not a book about leaders at the top – 'big L' leaders. It is more about those who are 'leading *in* the organisation' rather than those 'leading *the* organisation' – our 'little l' leaders. So where do they fit in? What is the impact of all the above on those 'managers who lead' and those 'leaders who manage' up, down and across organisations?

It is this. Top leaders have to grapple with the organisational response to the trends that matter for their organisations. They are the fulcrums for externally driven strategic change. But our 'little l' leaders' missions are different. They are the fulcrums for small-scale change – driven internally by those decisions made by the senior leadership of the firm. The decisions made by senior leadership set the context at a behavioural level for leadership that is widely distributed through the organisation.

What does this mean? It means that decisions made about strategy set the context for the way out 'little l' leaders form and articulate their business visions. It means that decisions made about culture and values set the context for the way out 'little l' leaders gain and sustain people's commitment and engagement. It means that decisions made about organisational structure, systems and processes set the context for the way our 'little l' leaders go about execution – making things happen. In short, the red thread runs from the trends identified in the external environment, through the decisions made by senior leaders to the way leadership throughout the organisation *behaves*. Behaviour is, by definition, business-driven and reward tends to mirror the behaviours that people think the business expects. At any point, misalignment can occur and when it does the organisation is likely to become dysfunctional. It is a fragile system.

The readings that follow are intended to provide food for thought as well as an incentive for action at the level at which the reader operates. We start with a series of reading around 'perspectives of leadership' to provoke readers into thinking about what leadership means to them. With this as a backdrop, we move onto issues relating to 'leading and sustaining high performance'. The third facet, 'making the team work' focuses on the vital topic of leadership teams. Next comes a series of readings entitled 'creating the future' – the important role creativity and innovation play in organisations. The last facet deals with execution both at corporate and individual levels – 'making things happen'. Finally, there is an appendix chapter, slightly technical, that provides a working model of 'effective organisational leadership' which stresses the contribution 'little l' leaders make in shaping the climate in which employees are either motivated and committed to perform, or not.

2

Perspectives on Leadership

The readings that follow explore leadership from a number of perspectives. If one thing is certain it is that there is no shortage of models, frameworks and views about what constitutes leadership. In our experience, however, most of the features found in the various leadership models and frameworks cluster into four overarching categories of what leaders need 'to be and do'. Figure 1 illustrates a framework we refer to as Effective Organisational Leadership (EOL).

What is Effective Organisational Leadership?

The inner ring and the three segments represent 42 personal leadership behaviours, either individually or in the aggregate for the leadership team. These are identifiable practices that can be assessed to determine how effective leaders are both in carrying out each component of the inner rings – creating vision, building and sustaining commitment, ensuring execution – and in balancing their personal behaviours among them.

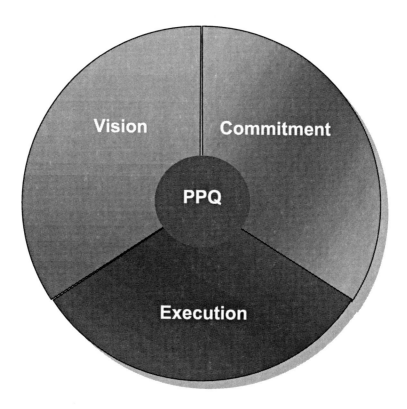

Figure 1: Effective Organisational Leadership (EOL)

Creating Vision

Effective leaders have a broad sense of direction, a vision, that others can share to unify their efforts. It represents a clear view of how the units for which a leader is responsible can contribute to the strategy of the whole. Vision consists of three elements that reflect the leader's sense of external opportunities, ways in which internal resources can be mobilised to capitalise on them and the leader's personal role (self) in that process.

Leaders who operate with a sense of vision demonstrate to others an orientation to marketplace trends, an understanding of how to get things done effectively within the organisation and how to get the most out of the capabilities of the business. They also demonstrate an excitement and determination about achieving the broader mission of the business. They ensure that daily activities are pursued and that decisions are made in the context of the broader goals.

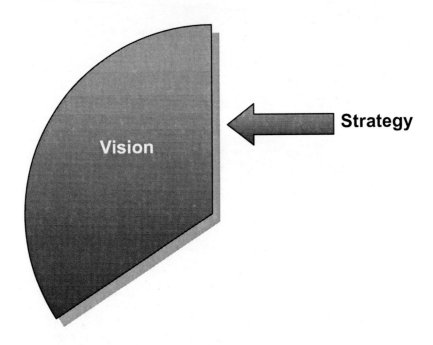

Figure 2: Vision Component of EOL Framework

At different levels in the organisation, as Figure 2 illustrates, a leader's personal vision will be shaped by the broader direction and strategy of the business. Ensuring alignment between these – what we refer to as 'Little V' and 'Big V' – is key to organisational success.

Building and Sustaining Commitment

Commitment is the engine that generates implementation energy from others. It reflects the leader's ability to get others excited about and dedicated to turning the vision into a reality. While a leader has or creates vision, commitment is an 'emotional buy-in response' elicited from others.

Leaders who are skilled at building and sustaining commitment do so primarily through five types of practices:

- **Communicating** with others to share information and elicit their views.
- **Involving** others in key activities and decisions.
- **Supporting** others through resource allocation and by managing external factors that threaten to frustrate their efforts.
- **Influencing** others to integrate their priorities with the broader vision.
- **Promoting** teamwork to leverage the strengths of the organisation in meeting customer needs.

For an organisation to successfully implement a strategy the leader's vision needs to have been shared with others in a way that builds conviction that the strategy will both work and benefit them.

As Figure 3 shows, a leader's ability to generate commitment shapes and is shaped by the broader culture of the organisation. The achievement of high levels of commitment depends both on articulating the values of the organisation and on valuing the contributions of others.

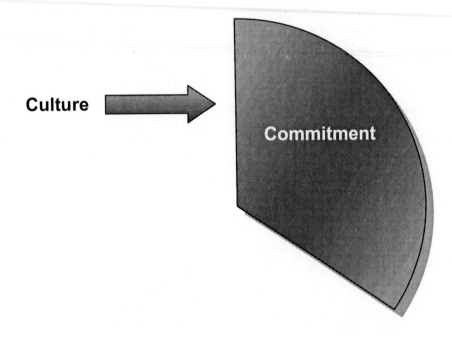

Figure 3: Commitment Component of EOL Framework

Ensuring Execution

Leadership involves not only vision to set broad direction and commitment to gain buy-in from the organisation but also the ability to influence the performance of others to ensure that the desired results are achieved. Ensuring execution prevents vision from becoming ethereal and commitment from becoming a love-in.

While vision sets the direction for the organisation and commitment provides the fuel for strategy implementation, execution represents the discipline that focuses the organisation's ideas and energy to getting things done.

Ensuring execution over the long term requires the willingness and ability of the leader to build the capability of others by actively managing their performance and fostering their professional growth.

By coaching others on how to learn from their experiences, encouraging innovation and providing assignments that 'stretch' people's capabilities, leaders foster organisational learning that increases the ability of the business to achieve results.

Structures, Systems & Procedures

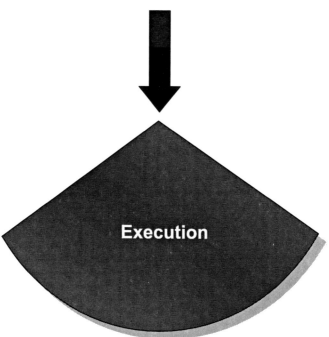

Figure 4: Execution Component of EOL Framework

Generally, the broader structures and systems of the organisation (e.g. reward, performance management, IT) influence ensuring execution behaviours. To the extent that a leader's vision or a new strategy requires significantly different behaviours from those that were appropriate in the past, management tools and broader planning and control systems may require significant modification to facilitate implementation. Alignment is the key.

Execution is essentially about *management*: the planning, organising and controlling that occurs through a well-developed performance management process. Management, in this sense, is therefore a component of effective organisational leadership rather than a separate function. In other words, we do not need to contrast 'leaders' and 'managers'. Leaders need to manage and managers need to lead. How this is accomplished is touched on in the last section of this chapter.

Personal/Professional Qualities

Central to effective leadership, and therefore the innermost core of the EOL Model, are the personal and professional qualities of the leader. While vision, commitment and execution are primarily focused on how executives lead others, personal/professional qualities represent the leader's ability to be a role model. Effective leaders possess a personal integrity that inspires trust. They demonstrate in their behaviours the high performance standards they expect of others. They continually seek to improve themselves. They encourage and facilitate similar improvement in their people and their business. In short, as the quotation from scholar Warren Bennis indicates, the *character* of the leader is right at the heart of effective organisational leadership.

"Let me state a personal bias that leadership is really a matter of character. The process of becoming a leader is no different from the process of becoming a fully integrated, healthy human being." (*Human Resource Executive*, December 1996)

The personal and professional qualities of leaders also reflect the need to manage the dilemmas and apparent contradictions inherent in the leadership role. Dilemmas between results and people, between short and long term, between profit and care for the environment. How able leaders are in managing these dilemmas depends in large part upon their personal/professional qualities. In modern leadership thinking, character is as important as capability and it cannot be learned.

Relative Balance in Leadership Behaviours

Balance between vision, commitment, execution and personal/ professional qualities is critical to effective organisational leadership. This balance ensures that the vision remains grounded in reality, that key players are on board and that results are achieved in a focused and disciplined manner.

Think of organisations that you know. Score them High, Medium and Low for Vision, Commitment and Execution? Are they high on Vision and low on Execution, like Apple was once in its history? Or they low on Vision and high on Execution like Ford was once in its history. Or are they low on Vision and Execution but high on Commitment because they are riding on the goodwill of their committed employees?

If the behaviours of individual executives are not in balance, and so often they are not, then this is likely to be reflected in the organisation's culture (a 'visionary' culture, a 'people' culture or an 'execution' culture). It then becomes the job of the leadership team to provide the balance required taking into account the stage of development the organisation has reached.

Which is why highly effective leaders need to have the courage to appoint members who are not mirror images of themselves but who will question, challenge and debate their views. Barrack Obama, the recently appointed US President, is a role model for this.

READING 1

One more time – leadership and management – are they the same or different?

Dr Mike Young & Professor Vic Dulewicz

- "Many organisations are over-led and under-managed."

- "Strong leadership with weak management is worse than the reverse."

- "The real challenge is to combine strong leadership and strong management and use each to balance the other."

- "Management is about coping with complexity. Leadership is about coping with change."

All well known quotations from John Kotter, the Harvard Business School leadership guru.

Reading 1 summarises an award-winning piece of research carried out by Commander (Dr) Mike Young and Professor Victor Dulewicz at Henley Management College. Published in the College's *Working Paper Series* (HWP 0510)* and accepted for publication by the *British Journal of Management*, the research, based on data from a sample of 261 Officers and Ratings (Sailors) in the Royal Navy, provides an illuminating insight into the differences between leadership and management.

The idea in brief – the 'core' idea

Much of the literature argues the difference between leadership and management suggesting that people cannot *both* manage *and* lead. *Either* you are a manager *or* leader but you are unlikely to be both.

This research support's Kotter's assertion that businesses should ignore the literature that says individuals cannot manage and lead.

While leadership and management can be differentiated the number of competencies common to both suggest that *effective performers tend to be both good leaders and good managers.* In other words, they possess competencies that enable them to demonstrate a balanced combination of leadership and management which is exactly what is required in the complex and changing world of the 21st Century.

Refreshingly, this finding aligns with the view that organisational effectiveness is not attributable to a single leader but is the outcome of effective collaboration across a broad range of leaders at different levels in the organisation.

The idea expanded – key findings

Both leadership and management involve four **supra-competencies**:

- Conceptualising – grasping and sharing the big picture
- Aligning – focusing on controllable activities by taking responsibility for converting plans into action
- Interacting – working with and through people
- Creating success – making a habit of delivering results

These four clusters have been shown to predict overall performance as well as effective leadership and management. **An individual endowed with them all has the potential to be both an effective leader and manager.**

Each of the supra-clusters comprises specific competencies. Many were common to both leadership and management, hence the core finding cited above. Others were unique to leadership or management. All are measurable using the psychometric instruments used in the research.

Leadership's unique contribution to overall performance comprised competencies that related primarily to **emotional factors,** e.g. displaying emotion clearly, thus reflecting the full spectrum of human drives and desires.

In contrast, management's unique contribution reflected a more **impersonal, task focus** , e.g. conscientiousness, which brings order and consistency to complex operations.

While this clearly provides evidence for the difference between management and leadership, the number of competencies *in common* to both suggest that effective performers possess competencies that enable them to demonstrate a balanced combination of leadership and management. **Effective performers in this study tended to be both good leaders and good managers.** Being a leader-manager is perhaps not such an inept title.

Motivation emerged as the single most important predictor of performance and was the only characteristic that significantly differentiated top from bottom performers. (By motivation the researchers mean having 'drive and energy to achieve clear results').

Motivation also accounted for most of the variation in assessments of leadership in the Royal Navy sample. Thriving on activity by being vigorous, ambitious and enjoying working to demanding goals and targets highlighted the importance of **energy and drive** in the leadership equation.

Displaying emotion clearly was the competency that most distinguished the superior from the below-average performers further emphasising the importance of emotion in leadership.

When it comes to management **motivation** also accounted for a significant amount of variance between high and low performers but **forward thinking** and **vision and imagination** (somewhat surprisingly) emerged as the most important management competencies.

The finding that **motivation** was the most significant predictor of overall performance and leadership and management effectiveness highlights its importance as a competency. **The most important ingredient for outstanding performance appears to be the desire to use one's competencies to the full.**

Finally, the existence of a number of competencies in the leadership domain that did not relate to performance raise the danger of rewarding the **image of leadership** when this may not be supported by actual performance.

* Adapted from the original Henley Working Paper (HWP 0510) and published with permission.

The idea in practice – putting the idea to work

The practical implications? What one thing can I implement as a result of this research?

As an organisation:

Review your leadership competency framework:

- Are you emphasising 'leadership at the expense of management' or 'management at the expense of leadership' as opposed to a balanced contribution from both?
- Is it sufficiently fine-tuned to reflect the emotional contribution required for effective leadership?
- Are there competencies that relate more to the image than the substance of leadership, i.e. performance?

As an individual:

- What is the balance between leadership and management that your role really requires? (Put %s on it). How does that compare with your current split? What does your team think? (Are you over-leading/under-managing of vice-versa?)
- To what extent are you emphasising the impersonal/task at the expense of the emotional? What will you do about it? How?
- Do you know whether you are leader or manager oriented? Find out by going to www.oedconsulting.com Click on Leadership Tools then Effective Organisational Leadership (EOL) and complete the online questionnaire to find out.

Go to http://www.henley.reading.ac.uk for more information about the Henley Working Paper (HWP) series.

READING 2

Two contrasting views of leadership

Professor Henry Minzberg & Frank Brown

This Reading summarises two contrasting views of leadership published in the *Financial Times* on 23 October 2006 – the views of Professor Henry Mintzberg (Insead and McGill) on the one hand and Frank Brown (formerly global leader at PWC and now Dean at Insead) on the other.

The idea in brief – the 'core' idea

The Mintzberg view...

Mintzberg's foghorn message is that separating leadership from management causes problems. By focusing on a single person, often obsessively, leadership becomes part of the cult of individuality that is sweeping the world and undermining organisations in particular and communities in general. In essence, what business requires in the future is less leadership and more community-ship.

The Brown view...

Brown argues in contrast that the last thing business needs is more managers. On the contrary, it is in need of leaders prepared to challenge rather than simply listen and execute. This means chief executives building leadership strength deep in their organisations rather than surrounding themselves with 'mirror image managers'. In essence, what business requires in the future is more transcultural leaders and less managers.

The idea expanded – key findings

Mintzberg:

- **Separating leadership from management is part of the problem.** In the same way that no one really wants to work for a manager who has had a leadership bypass so no one wants to work for a leader who is managerially impotent. What business requires is some plain, ordinary 'leader/managers'.

- Micro managing, the soothsayers and nitpickers so derided by Jack Welch, are not in demand (*Ed: despite the high control scores of many managers we meet*). **But equally damaging can be the big-picture macro managers – the ones who sit up there pronouncing great visions, grand strategies and abstract performance standards while everyone else scuttles around 'implementing'.**

- Mintzberg labels this **'leadership apart'** and says there is too much of it around – the hyped-up, individually focused, context-free leadership so popular in the one place which has never created real leaders and never will – the business school classroom.

- **Leadership grows in context, where it gains 'legitimacy'.** Mostly these days we get illegitimate leadership – selected by outsiders (e.g. external directors) and imposed on insiders. How remarkable that those who know the candidates best – those who have been led by them – rarely get consulted on these choices. True leadership is earned. How many of today's companies (and countries) can claim to be headed by people with that kind of legitimacy?

- People, of course, seek leaders. But often they fool themselves by confusing leaders with leadership. **There is a need for more of what has been called 'distributed leadership'** – roles that are fluid and shared by various people at different levels in the organisation (*Ed: what OED calls 'little l leadership'*).

- Mintzberg goes further. He believes (*Ed: are professors supposed to 'believe?'*) that **leadership resides in the community** and that our obsession with leadership causes us to build organisations that are over-dependent on individual initiative (the heroic leadership syndrome). In short, by dividing people into leaders and followers we do not allow organisations to function as communities. So when they fail we blame the leader and go out and get another one.

- **The cult of leadership has gone too far.** What should be gone, argues Mintzberg, is this magic bullet of the individual as the solution to the world's problems. "In four years (Lou) Gerstner has added more than $40bn to IBM's share value" proclaimed Fortune magazine. All by himself! **We don't need only better leadership we also need less leadership.** The very use of the word leadership tilts thinking toward the individual and away from the community.

Brown:

- The concept of leadership must not be confined to the 'headliners' – **it must be a concept with the potential to include and apply to everyone**, the person occupying the corner office as well as the person rising fast through the divisional ranks.

- But that is not to say that everyone will become a leader but rather that everyone does and can possess some leadership qualities. Organisations need leaders at every level not simply at the top. **This means that leadership training should not start on the job but at a much earlier stage in an executive's career cycle.**

- In complete contrast with Mintzberg, Brown holds that **training people to be leaders must be one of the main pursuits of business schools**, that MBA students should not only earn a degree but they should also earn leadership. Business school programmes should be breeding grounds for global leaders.

- **The business world does not just need more leaders it needs more transcultural leaders,** people who possess the knowledge and sensitivity to operate anywhere in the world. Too often, western models of business have been forced on other cultures. What works better is patience, an ability to listen, to build consensus and get along in another culture.

- **How do we develop more transcultural leaders?** Brown proposes first by creating more culturally diverse educational communities (at business schools) and secondly by going beyond classroom learning and focusing on experiential learning as a critical training ground.

- B-schools will need to continue to enhance efforts to provide the real world experience that is essential to developing individuals as great leaders.

- Fast-forward 10 years and we will no longer see a business world defined by a western-dominated corporate culture. **The rise of Asia, Latin America and Eastern Europe will create new corporate norms, organisations and business executives.** Those who will succeed in this new order are not capable managers successful at executing business norms and practices but leaders who are able to forge new business paradigms in a world where the balance of power has shifted.

- **This transcultural leadership will be earned not inherited.** The corporate and educational worlds will need to think beyond the traditional parameters to help breed a generation capable of leading organisations in this new world not just managing them.

The idea in practice – putting the idea to work

The practical implications? What one thing can I implement as a result of this research?

- (*The Mintzberg case*) Challenge every single speech, programme, and communication in your organisation that uses the word 'leadership' that does not give equal attention to 'community-ship'. What are the implications and possible actions?

- (*The Brown case*) Challenge every single piece of leadership training and development to assess the extent to which transcultural issues are addressed. What are the implications and possible actions?

- (*For yourself*) Which of the two perspectives are you naturally inclined to? Why? Is this the same as your organisation's perspective? If not, what are you going to do about it?

READING 3

Why should anyone be led by you?

Rob Goffee and Gareth Jones

The article *'Why Should Anyone Be Led by you?'* first appeared in the *Harvard Business Review* in October-November 2000. In 2006 the much anticipated book under the same title (with the added sub-title *'What It Takes to Be an Authentic Leader'*) by the same authors (Rob Goffee and Gareth Jones) was published to wide acclaim by the Harvard Business School Press (permission gained for this adapted excerpt). Along with Jim Collins' *Good to Great*, John Kotter's *A Force for Change* (and his other works) and Kouses & Posner's *The Leadership Challenge* it probably ranks among the forefront of recent additions to the leadership reading list. This **Reading** provides an outline of the book's 245 very readable, story-filled pages.

The idea in brief – the 'core' idea

The provocative title of the book comes from a question that the authors have asked frequently at leadership seminars over the past five years: *why should anyone be led by you?* (Legend has it that the question was first asked by Greg Dyke when Director-General of the BBC in a quest to radically change that organisation's culture; if executives could not answer the question during the time they were in the shower then spending more time with their families might be a better use of their time).

For Goffee and Jones, effective leadership is grounded first and foremost in 'authenticity', the central theme that winds its way through the nine chapters and two appendices of the book. To quote from the *Financial Times* review of the book: "Successful leaders are those who behave genuinely, who show themselves warts and all, rather than pretending to be something they are not...leaders who lack integrity are suffering from a fatal flaw." Or to quote the authors themselves: "Copy-cat leadership will never result in another Jack Welch or Richard Branson. What organisations need – and what followers want – are authentic leaders who know who they are, where the organisation needs to go and how to convince followers to help them take it there."

Three fundamental axioms about leadership underpin Goffee and Jones' research: first, leadership is *situational* – there is no one style and no universal traits; secondly, leadership is *non-hierarchical* – it may or may not exist at the most senior levels of the organisation. It is certainly not the preserve of the few. Great organisations have leaders at all levels. Thirdly, leadership is *relational* – you cannot be a leader without followers and having followers requires relationship-building skills often not provided by the strategic and analytical focus of some of the major business schools.

The idea expanded – key findings

While the authors take great care not to present their findings as a 'recipe for good leadership' in the interests of digestibility we distil six key themes that form the backbone of the book. Each of these is summarised below:

Theme 1: Be Yourself – More – with Skill

- You must be *yourself*. People want to be led by a person not a role holder or position filler or administrator.
- Be yourself *in context*. Leadership does not take place in a vacuum. Effective leaders are able to read the context and respond accordingly. They do this without losing their authenticity.
- Act as a leader – knowing when to 'act close' (create empathy) and when to act 'distant' (create edge). And how to get the balance and the timing right.
- Most importantly, you must also *want* to lead. Do you?

Theme 2: Know and Show Yourself – Enough

To be yourself, you must *know* yourself and *show* yourself – enough to maximise your leadership impact. What does this mean?

- Develop a close understanding of what is different about you – *what works for you with others*. Learn to use these genuine differences to serve both your own and the team's interests.
- Try things out and get honest feedback from colleagues, family and friends. Experiment. Seek new experiences. Move outside your comfort zone. Do not become a slave to routines.
- Know where you have come from and how it relates to who you are and what you do. Explore your biography. Ask yourself searching questions about your background and upbringing. Return to your roots. Spend time with people who know you as you are.

Theme 3: Take Personal Risks

Leadership is for a purpose. It is not a friendship contest. Effective leaders *care* about their purpose and goals enough to reveal their authentic selves. Revealing your authentic self means taking personal risks so:

- Be prepared to show your foibles. Put a little bit of yourself on the line. Let others see you are human too.
- Distinguish between a real weakness you reveal and a fatal flaw (i.e. central to task performance) you do not.
- Be selective. Don't focus so much on revealing weaknesses that they drown out your strengths. Keep it in context. Do it 'enough'.

Theme 4: Read – and Rewrite – the Context

Leadership is always contextual. There is no notion of a universal leadership formula. Effective leaders develop *situation-sensing skills* so as to form the right judgements and make the best decisions possible. They know when it feels right.

What do leaders need to be able to sense?

Key individuals – *those who make the biggest performance impact.*
- Use informal means to collect data ('going for a coffee').
- Use indirect rather than direct questions ('What if…').
- Ask about non-work activities ('Why do you enjoy…').
- Take time. Build a picture. Seek to understand.

Important teams that the leader must be involved in to get things done.
- Balance task and relationship behaviours ('do business then get to know each other' v 'get to know each other then do business').
- Build in time for people to relate to each other (often overlooked).
- Foster diversity in the team to encourage innovation. (squeezed out by the pressure to become 'mean and lean').

With remote teams, establish face-to-face relationships before relying on other means of communicating (most human beings are hardwired for sociability).

The organisation itself
- Conform *enough* to establish the critical connections necessary to deliver *change* (minimal acceptance is required before change can begin).
- Balance both sociability (affective relationships at work) and solidarity (task-focused co-operation). Communal cultures (for example, Apple, Microsoft, Google) tend to be high on both. Read the situation for the mix required.
- Tease rather than freeze or please – that is, retain authenticity but acquire enough of the behaviours in the new situation to operate effectively.

Theme 5: Manage Social Distance

Effective leaders move skilfully from closeness to distance and back again. They are able to get close yet paradoxically keep their distance. They empathise yet provide edge.

- *Establish closeness* to get to know the individuals concerned and for the individuals to know you. By being close we show who we are. It offers a context for disclosure – of weakness as well as strength. But avoid premature or inappropriate closeness (for example, over-focusing on closeness at the expense of performance – being 'one of them')

(Introverts tend to find establishing closeness more difficult. This is a significant issue since they are over-represented at top levels in organisations. As Goffee and Jones point out we need a 'Leadership Guide for Introverts')

- *Establish distance* to signal an overarching purpose or goal or to address a performance issue. Norms, values and standards are non-negotiable. Leadership is not an end in itself but a means. Establishing distance enables the leader to build solidarity with followers based on a common purpose.

  (Be distant when you are setting out the 'what' – be close when you are discussing the 'how'.)

Getting the balance wrong will fail to achieve authenticity. Better to overdo distance first (like the new teacher). Even while being close the leader should reserve a degree of her/himself. Both need to feel the edgy potential of distance.

Leadership is not about being nice. Leaders are the stewards of the overriding purpose or goal of the organisation. From that they derive their authority.

Theme 6: Communicate – with Care

Skilful leaders ensure they use the right mode of communication. Choosing how to communicate is a mini-case study of how you can effectively *be yourself, in context, with skill.* Bear in mind:

- Choosing the right *channel* – while face-to-face is always critical connecting with larger audiences is also important for senior leaders.
- Choosing the right *content* – so as to energise rather than just inform. Compelling narratives – stories – are needed to touch

peoples' emotions. People are rarely energised by dense, power point slides.

- Choosing *pace and tempo* to match the channel and reflect the content.

Conclusion (If there is one?)

Goffee and Jones hold to the view that successful leadership is *situational* (as well as non-hierarchical and relational): that is, responding and adapting appropriately to time and place. To be an adaptable yet authentic leader requires considerable skill.

While leadership training and coaching cannot – and should not – help with a person's core authenticity, it can help leaders to become better, to 'be themselves – *with skill*'.

The idea in practice – putting the idea to work

The practical implications? What one thing can I implement a result of this research?

The book was based on the simplest of questions: *'why should anyone be led by YOU?'* Like all simple questions the answers are often not so simple. Take the customary blank piece of paper and in one succinct sentence answer the question in a way that a six-year-old child could readily understand.

NOW turn the piece of paper over and answer the following:

- What personal differences could form the basis of your leadership capability?
- Which personal weaknesses could you reveal to those you are leading?
- Which critical skill do you need to develop to be yourself more skilfully?

READING 4

Enabling bold visions

Jay A Conger & Douglas A Ready

We've all been there. Three days at a leadership team offsite to craft a new vision for the business. No shortage of commitment and generally a buzz of excitement by the time people pack their bags for the trip home. The leader feels good, the team members feel good and if there is one the professional facilitator also feels good.

Months later, the buzz has worn off as reality intrudes as it usually does. In short, following the initial enthusiasm the business leadership was having a hard time reconciling the new vision with day-to-day reality. The gap between inspiration and implementation remained large.

Jay A Conger and Douglas A Ready ('Enabling Bold Visions', *MIT Sloan Management Review*, Winter 2008*) set out to find out why and what business leaders and their teams might do to turn bold visions into operational realities by conducting research in 40 global organisations to determine a best-practice model.

Reading 4 summarises the findings from this research.

The idea in brief – the 'core' idea

Companies that successfully put new visions of the enterprise into practice follow a process that takes the organisation through five phases.

In today's competitive landscape, this tends to be an iterative process reflecting the fact that most companies will need to update or change their visions more regularly than in the past – or at the very minimum, check that they are still appropriate rather than assume they are. First, however, the authors identify some reasons why some visions fail to get off the ground.

Why bold visions derail

New visions can fade away for many apparently unique reasons. The authors categorised these reasons into six themes:

- *Failure to focus* – allowing the vision to become mired in a haze of other priorities – i.e. initiative overload.
- *Sitting out the dance* – explaining the vision but not engaging a partner to make it work – i.e. not communicating to others in the business the steps to the new dance.
- *Skipping skill building* – failing to identify and develop the skills that would be needed to support the vision – i.e. force-fitting the new vision onto the existing infrastructure.
- *Mismatching messages and metrics* – reinforcing business as usual by continuing to practise yesterday's behaviours – i.e. failing to demonstrate new mindsets and behaviours which signal 'life has changed around here'.
- *Clashing powers* – allowing powerful groups to ring-fence core activities that belong in the past – i.e. because the new vision threatens the supremacy of the old guard.
- *Neglecting the talent pipeline* – failing to prepare people deep in the organisation who can act as effective change agents – i.e. who embody the behaviours and values of the new call to action.

These six problem areas explain why many bold visions fail to produce measurable change. **But according the authors a model of change can help companies to avoid this trap.**

The idea expanded – key findings

Conger & Ready observed **five critical activities**, performed in sequence, that together form a systems approach to enabling bold visions – in essence, a framework for leading large-scale organisation change initiatives:

Phase 1: Framing the agenda

The leaders in the study successfully brought about change by

framing their organisation's challenges as compelling stories that created an urgent agenda for change.

On one axis, they couched the agenda in terms of both **present and future performance** – both the company's future growth strategy and its current customer value proposition. This reflected the company's focus on 'doing.'

On the other axis, they couched the agenda in terms of both **external and internal stakeholders** – both the way customers and others perceived the new vision and the way its employees perceived the climate of change. This reflected the company's focus on 'being'.

(The authors cite the BBC's new enterprise agenda: Creative Future, as an example. In order to drive performance the BBC would invest heavily in digital technology and become leaner and smaller. In order to create the climate to deliver these objectives the corporation's leaders would become more agile and collaborative).

Phase 2: Engaging the organisation

Once change leaders have framed their agendas they must do whatever they can **to distribute ownership as broadly as possible**.

Bold visions, say the authors, must be **enabled rather than executed**. This reflects the fact that while many managers yearn for stronger leadership they want a different style, one characterised by authentic collaboration and broad-based engagement.

Bold visions are likely to 'frighten the horses' so leaders need to understand this by making sure those who have succeeded under yesterday's business model don't become enemies of the new vision. They do this through **skilful involvement**.

(In the BBC this was achieved by bringing together teams from the different BBC groups to work through the details of how the BBC would transform itself from a collection of separate units to a unified organisation that relied on cross-unit collaboration).

Phase 3: Building mission-critical capabilities

While engagement with the new vision is necessary it is not sufficient. The **development of new capabilities** is also necessary as usually companies have gaps in what they want to do and what they can do.

There are both practical and political considerations to consider which it will be easier to do if the phases outlined here are followed sequentially. **It is difficult for any leader to have a serious conversation about building new capabilities without first framing the agenda and engaging people in active dialogue.**

(The BBC attacked these problems in a variety of ways. The sum of these ways was a newly skilled base of employees who could work across platforms and who had a deep understanding of digital media).

Phase 4: Creating alignment

Bold visions rarely flounder because of full-frontal attacks. Sabotage tends to be subtler and sometimes includes 'own goals' when executives communicate unintentional messages.

Companies and their employees are hardwired to resist change. This will be even more so when companies that are trying to enact 'one company' visions continue to measure and reward mangers on their ability to meet unit objectives.

The message is clear and simple: both structure and processes need to be aligned with the vision if change is to happen.

(The BBC created a new Operations Group to bring leadership, direction and consistency to the BBC's big infrastructure projects, a critical element of the Creative Future vision).

Phase 5: Energising the organisation

Clearly, no vision can come to life without the enthusiastic support and follow-through of literally thousands of managers and employees.

In the study, however, it was found that often companies did not have the talent to see the vision through to completion.

This finding led the authors to conclude that **leadership failures were not so much a matter of struggling individuals but inattention to the connections between talent requirements and capability requirements**. "All too often the problem is not that leaders are failing their companies but rather that a company's talent policies are failing its leaders."

(In the BBC, a new head of BBC People was brought in with the express purpose and mandate to create a people strategy that was directly linked to the corporation's Creative Future vision. All division heads engaged in and signed off on the strategy).

* Adapted excerpts from Enabling Bold Visions by Jay A Conger and Douglas A Ready, MIT Sloan Management Review (Winter 2008) by permission of publisher.

The idea in practice – putting the idea to work

The practical implications? What one thing can I implement as a result of this research?

The five-phase model was developed with CEOs in mind and used reference organisations such as the BBC, Nissan and Deutsche Bank.

But the approach (in this author's view) is equally applicable to **smaller scale organisational components** – the business units, functions and geographies that comprise all large enterprises.

For the part of the organisation for which you are responsible:

1. Give a score out of 10 for the extent to which each phase of the model has been successfully implemented – e.g. To what extent are people fully engaged with the vision?

2. What do your scores tell you about the need for change in your part of the organisation? What will you now do?

READING 5

Organisational climate and leadership styles

Daniel Goleman (in part)

Reading 5 links two seminal pieces of research: research into *organisational climate* first conducted in a Harvard Business School classroom in the late 1960s (Litwin & Stringer 1968) and research into *leadership styles* conducted more recently by Hay/McBer (2000). The links are partially but well summarised by Daniel Goleman in Leadership that gets Results (*Harvard Business Review*, March-April 2000 – permission gained for this adapted excerpt).

The idea in brief – the 'core' idea

The Harvard climate research identified six key factors (see below) that influence an organisation's working environment: 'how it feels to work around here'.

Having the right climate profile produced **three measurable effects**: it increased employee motivation, employee development and retention and employee performance.

The research also identified **three key determinants** of climate: leadership practices, organisation culture and organisation structure, systems and procedures.

Much research (including the author's own – see Reading 1) has demonstrated the link between leadership practices and climate. What the Hay/Mcber research did was to categorise the key variable, leadership practices, into **six leadership styles** (see below) each based on specific components of emotional intelligence.

The bottom line of the research was to show that **leaders who used styles that positively affected the climate had decidedly better financial results than those who did not**. More specifically, leaders who mastered four of these styles had the best climate and business performance.

The idea expanded – key findings

The six organisational climate factors

Since the original research, a number of variations have been used. In the research referred to above. The six factors are:

- *Flexibility* – how free employees feel to innovate unencumbered by rules, procedures and red tape.
- The sense of *responsibility* the employee has towards the organisation – being empowered and not having to double check decisions with others.
- The level of *standards* that people set in terms of performance expectations, quality and pride in 'work well done'.
- *Reward and recognition* in terms of the feeling of being rewarded – both monetarily and otherwise – for a job well done.
- The *clarity* people have about roles, responsibilities and priorities.
- The level of *commitment* to the organisation, its purpose and its goals.

These six factors can be regarded as a snapshot of any part of the organisation in the 'here and now'. This differs from culture that tends to be an organisation-wide phenomenon shaped by 'leaders at the top'. Climate is more local, more shaped by immediate leaders through the practices they adopt.

The six leadership styles

The research showed that leaders used six leadership styles each springing from different components of emotional intelligence. They are:

- The *coercive* style – 'do what I tell you' approach from leaders who demand immediate compliance (often useful in a crisis or turnaround situation).
- The *authoritative* style – 'come with me' approach from leaders who mobilise people towards a vision (useful when change is needed or a clear direction required).

- The *affiliative* style – 'people come first' approach from leaders who create harmony and build emotional bonds (appropriate when rifts need to be healed or the situation is stressful)
- The *democratic* style – 'what do you think?' approach from leaders who forge consensus through participation and involvement (useful when input is required from employees or team consensus needed).
- The *pacesetting* style – 'do as I do, now' approach from leaders who set high standards for performance (handy when quick results from a highly motivated team are required).
- The *coaching* style – 'try this' approach from leaders who focus on developing people for the future.

Key findings

All six leadership styles have a measurable effect on each aspect of climate. However, the research indicated that of the six styles **the authoritative one is most effective, driving up every aspect of climate**. And because of its positive impact the authoritative style appears to work well in any business situation. But it is particularly relevant when a business is adrift and the leader needs to chart a new course to which people are committed.

Three other styles follow closely behind: *affiliative, democratic* and *coaching*. The most effective leaders are those who can master these four styles and be able to switch flexibly between them as needed.

Summary

A strong link exists between individual and organisational performance and particular climate profiles. Local leaders can shape climate through their leadership practices (which may be more potent than an organisation's culture). Leadership practices can be distilled into six styles each reflecting a combination of emotional intelligence components. Mastering four of these styles and applying them appropriately will lead to more productive climates and therefore to increased employee motivation, employee development and retention and employee performance.

The idea in practice – putting the idea to work

The practical implications? What one thing can I implement as a result of this research?

1. Rate yourself 1-10 on each of the six styles. If you score 8+ you have 'mastery'.
2. Consider the most likely contexts you operate in. Is your repertory big enough? If not, which style(s) do you need to develop?
3. (To do so in a sustainable way you will need to identify which emotional intelligence competencies underlie the leadership style you are lacking. For example, if you want to have a more affiliative style you may need to work on empathy and building relationship skills or communicating more effectively.)
4. Reflect on those around you. Which of your team members has the style(s) you lack? Use them!

READING 6

Leading business performance

Dr Fred Cannon

The focus of **Reading 6** is the relationship between three big organisational variables: *leadership practices, organisation culture and work unit (team) climate.* It is based on data collected and analysed in a global financial institution for doctoral research published in 2004. It attempts to answer the very practical question: how can leaders in organisations most effectively impact on their work environments to improve motivation, performance and productivity?

The idea in brief – the 'core' idea

Even in organisations with strong or even 'cult-like' cultures leadership practices can have a greater effect on 'the way it feels to work here' than the culture itself.

While in healthy cultures leaders need to be culture-carriers the research shows that going beyond this in terms of leadership practices will have a more significant impact on individual and organisational performance *because* the level of motivation and engagement is higher when the climate in which people work is 'fit for purpose'.

Obsession by leaders with culture in recent years has detracted from a more productive focus on building high-performance work units *at the level at which they are responsible.* Research going back to 1968 supports the proposition that high performance work climates result primarily from 'the way the leader leads'. This study unequivocally supports that proposition.

The idea expanded – key findings

Three myths need to be debunked before we get to the meat of the research findings:

Myth 1: *"Leadership and management are different."*

They are not.

Neither are they the same. The model underlying the study positions management (execution) as an integral part of effective organisational leadership.

Myth 2: *"The focal point should be the competence of the individual leader – usually the one at the top."*

Not true.

First, leadership has failed to keep pace with organisational design. The devolution of leadership capability and authority has lagged behind modern organisational architecture with flat structures and loose, innovative formats. This means we need more 'little l' and less 'big L' leadership. More, better leadership spread across fewer levels.

Secondly, the key is the team. As the CEO of Wal-Mart recently commented: "The team is key. You cannot *run* this company. You can lead it, but you cannot run it".

Mckinsey seem to agree: "The prize for building effective top teams is clear: they develop better strategies, perform more consistently and increase the confidence of stakeholders. They get positive results – and make the work itself a more positive experience both for the team's members and for the people they lead."

Thirdly, while leaders clearly need to be competent, equally important they need to have qualities. As the recently appointed principal of Henley Management College remarked: "because leadership is fundamentally about dilemmas and choices, character and integrity are as important as ability".

The model used in this research incorporated personal and professional qualities.

Myth 3: *"If we get the culture right everything else will follow."*

Partly true.

But we cannot always wait for the time it takes to get the culture right and even if we do the large-scale effort involved is often doomed.

Hence the distinction in this research between culture (remember the definition? "Values, beliefs and underlying assumptions") and climate ("The way it feels to work in *this part* of the organisation"). With great interest, at a seminar given recently to a major UK bank Warner Burke – one of the world's organisational scholars – floated the idea that 'the way to change culture is through changing climates'.

Interesting thought.

The key findings

What did the analysis of the views of 727 managers at different levels in one of the most highly regarded organisations in the world tell us?

- Leadership remains an important determinant of culture but in this research *less so.*
- *Both* the wider organisation culture and leadership practices significantly impact on local work unit (team) climate but *leadership practices* were the greatest determinant.
- The *people-related dimensions* of climate (for example, support, recognition) were impacted more significantly by leadership practices than task-related dimensions (for example, standards, responsibility).
- Both *transformational* and *transactional* leadership practices had a positive impact on the people-related dimensions of climate (in historical language good leadership *and* management have a positive effect on people).
- The leadership practices most commonly associated with a productive work climate were understanding the business environment, two-way communication and defining performance expectations.

- The aspects of organisation culture that impacted most significantly on climate were *performance and productivity* and *business focus.*

Whereas previous research had demonstrated that culture was twice as important as leadership practices this research showed that leadership practices were twice as important as culture in its effect on local work unit (team) climates and therefore on motivation and performance.

Leaders who foster a culture of performance and productivity and business focus, understand the business environment, practise two-way communications and shape and define expectations are more likely to create high-performance work units than those who focus solely on 'making the culture work'.

The idea in practice – putting the idea to work

The practical implications? What one thing can I implement a result of this research?

Among the many messages in the research working with the concept of climate is probably the most useful. What does this mean?

1. Focus on the unit for which the leader is responsible – the unit is simply defined as the leader and his/her direct reports.
2. Figure out what are the few key dimensions of climate that matter. This research used six generic measures from previous research but you and your team can identify your own (much better than teambuilding).
3. Conduct a team meeting to decide where the unit is now on each dimension. You can use a simple 1-10 scale. Then do the same but ask 'where should the unit be looking ahead?' Same scales. Use a large sheet stuck to the wall and flipchart pens.
4. Do a gap analysis. Where are the biggest gaps between current and desired? Look at the gap you perceive and the gap your direct reports perceive. If theirs is smaller – fine (unless they are low as well). If theirs is larger then a cause for concern.

5. Look at any differences between the views of the leaders and those of the direct reports. If the DRs have a more positive view – fine (unless the gap between their view of current and desired is large). If they have a more negative view then this is a cause for concern.

6. Now identify priorities. Focus on 2-3 dimensions people have most concern about. Problem-solve by brainstorming why a particular dimension gets a low score. Do a cause and effect exercise. Don't work on all the dimensions simultaneously – go for the 'biggest bang for the buck'.
   (Using the research's generic measures it is often best to tackle Vision or Clarity first. Then Standards and Recognition probably followed by Support and Responsibility. Finally Commitment.)

7. Agree specific action steps to close the gap between actual and desired. This may – and probably will – focus on the leader's behaviours. Be open. Be concrete. What behaviours need to change? How? Score them as before on a 1-10 scale and monitor progress over three months. Use the team as the leader's coach to build a higher performing team.

8. Make this process an ongoing part of your team's processes. The process itself will work wonders for team commitment.

For an academic summary of the research see *Working paper Series* (HWP 0409), Henley Management College www.henley.reading.ac.uk

READING 7

The neuroscience of leadership

Kaizen Training

In a recent Lucy Kellaway column (*Financial Times*) she explains why a visit to the dentist is more likely to produce a change in behaviour than many of the so-called change programmes that clutter many of today's large corporations. Changing behaviour is hard, even for individuals let alone organisations and even when new habits can mean the difference between life and death. For example, only one in nine patients it is claimed adopts healthier day-to-day habits after coronary bypass surgery. Changing behaviour is hard.

Businesses everywhere face this kind of problem: improvement and change isn't possible without altering the day-to-day behaviour of people. Yet we all know many leadership efforts and organisational change initiatives fail. Now, **breakthroughs in brain research can start to explain how to make individual and organisational change succeed.**

Reading 7 summarises a recent paper by Kaizen* www.kaizen-training.com which draws on the work of David Rock and Jeffrey Schwartz* to link findings from neuroscience with learning and change.

*David Rock: *Quiet Leadership – Six Steps to Transforming Performance at Work*, Collins 2006 and Personal Best, Simon & Schuster 2001

*Jeffrey Schwartz: *The Mind and the Brain* (with Sharon Begley), Regan Books 2002 and *Brain Lock – Free Yourself from Obsessive Compulsive Behaviour*, Regan Books 2002

The idea in brief – the 'core' idea

Managers who understand recent breakthroughs in cognitive science can lead and influence change more effectively – i.e. organisational transformation that takes into account the physiological nature of the brain and the ways it predisposes people to resist some forms of leadership and accept others. The paper explores *five conclusions* about organisational change that would have been considered downright wrong a few years ago and draws on these to help answer the question: **'How can leaders effectively change their own or other people's behaviour?'**

The idea expanded – key findings

- **Change is pain** – organisational change is unexpectedly difficult because it provokes physiological discomfort. In essence, this is to do with the nature of human memory – in particular a strange part of the brain called the basil ganglia – and other ways that the brain functions. The bottom line is that trying to change any hardwired habit requires a lot of effort and personal discomfort. No wonder the majority of training programmes fail even to get under the surface of what is required.

- **Behaviourism doesn't work** – many existing models for changing people's behaviour are drawn from a field called behaviourism (think Pavlov's dog). In essence, if you manipulate incentives and threats (carrot and stick) then the behaviour you seek will be forthcoming.

  Unfortunately, even where this is the case, it rarely sticks long term. Yet, despite the evidence to the contrary, the carrot and stick are alive and well in many organisations today.

- **Humanism is overrated** – when therapists and trainers left behind the carrot and stick to focus on empathy through a more person-centred approach they believed that getting people on board by establishing trust and rapport was the road to salvation. This warm bath approach assumes that if people receive the correct information about what they are doing wrong, and the right incentives are in place, they will automatically change for the better – i.e. do what you want.

Unfortunately, the human brain has a tendency to act like a two-year old – tell it what to do and it automatically pushes back. Neither the behaviourist nor the humanist approach is sophisticated enough to provide a reliable method for producing behaviour change in intelligent people even if it is in their own interest to change.

- **Focus is power** – cognitive scientists have known for 20 years that the brain is capable of significant internal change in response to environmental change. It is also known that the brain changes as a function of where an individual puts his or her attention. The power is the focus. Attention continually reshapes the patterns of the brain. So people who work in different silos and specialisms learn to think – and act – differently. They possess physiological differences that prevent them from seeing the world the same way.

- **Expectations shape reality** – people's mental maps, their theories, expectations and attitudes play a more central role in human perception than was previously understood. People experience what they expect to experience (think Pygmalion). So two people on the same customer service telephone line could hold two different mental maps of the same customer. While one might hear only childish complaints the other would hear valuable suggestions for improvement. It all depends on what you see – or rather want to see – through your experience-shaped lens.

* Published with permission from Kaizen Training Ltd.

The idea in practice – putting the idea to work

The practical implications? What one thing can I implement as a result of this research?

How, then, in the light of the above, do you go about facilitating change?

- The impact of mental maps suggests that one way is to start by *cultivating moments of insight*. Large-scale behaviour change requires a large-scale change in mental maps. This in turn requires some kind of event or experience that allows people to provoke themselves, in effect, to change their attitudes and expectations more quickly and dramatically than they normally would.
  (This is why employees need to own the change. It's not just a left over piece of humanism. The customer service clerk won't change the way s/he listens without a moment of insight in which her/his mental map shifts to seeing the customer as an expert rather than a child. Leaders wanting to change the way people think or behave need to recognise, encourage, and deepen both their own and other's insights.)

- For insights to be useful they need to be *generated from within* not served up on a plate. People need to make their own connections because everyone has a unique brain architecture (Socrates understood this). What's more, it is far more effective and efficient to help others come to their own insights.

- The more concentration and attention paid to a particular mental experience over a specific time the more likely it is the experience will become hardwired into the person's identity – i.e. become a habit. Which is probably why a training programme will increase productivity by 28% in contrast to follow-up coaching which achieves 88%.

How, then, can leaders effectively change their own or other people's behaviour?

- Start by *leaving problem behaviours in the past*. Focus on identifying and creating new behaviours. Use a solution-based questioning approach that facilitates self-insight rather than advice giving. In short, be the best coach you can!

- *Focus as much attention as possible on the smallest number of changes that will have the greatest impact.* Be selective, be focused and give positive feedback – not to be nice but to reinforce behaviour that is beginning to work and to act as a signal 'to do more of'.

- *Be creative and bold in designing interventions where people can picture the new behaviours in their own minds* and in the process discover new mental maps that have the potential to stick and therefore shape new outlooks and new behaviours.

Summary

It is now clear that human behaviour in the workplace doesn't work the way many executives think it does or should. Which is why the change efforts fall flat and probably why we have an exponential growth in executive coaching which, done well, reflects the principles described above.

Toyota saw it coming. Through innovative shop floor and meeting-room practices that resonate deeply with the innate pre-dispositions of the brain they achieved huge success. If the medics are to be believed, a fMRI scan of a Toyota employee's brain taken 10 years ago would show very different patterns to one taken today.

In the meantime, we stumble on hoping that by chance some of what we do just might stick. If we are lucky, that is.

READING 8

Are you a listening company?

Sunday Times Survey

If you look at a graph that shows the differing performances of the publicly-quoted businesses among the Sunday Times 100 Best Companies and those listed on the FTSE index you will see that compound returns over a five-year period show a 2.2% negative return for FTSE 100 companies against a 10.2% gain for the Best Companies. Over three years, the returns move to gains of 1.3% and 8.8% respectively.

Reading 8 looks behind the eight broad survey categories (66 questions) and 80,212 respondents across 449 companies to distil the *one key factor* that impacted on a company's final position in the 2004 rankings of best companies.

The idea in brief – the 'core' idea

In response to a series of statements across the eight categories, employees are asked to score them on a seven-point scale from 'strongly agree' to 'strongly disagree.' Ratings for the leadership, my manager, giving something back and personal growth categories increased significantly while those for well being, my team and fair deal fell.

While the overall positive score for company leadership rose from 69.3% to 70.1%, the factor score hid a wider range of responses on the quality of leadership in the 100 Best Companies. For example, a sharp rise in the positive score among employees for being inspired by the person leading their organisation (up from 65.5% to 68.3%) is balanced by an even sharper fall in the amount of faith they have in the leader (down from 75% to 71.2%).

In the survey the most revealing question asked whether *"senior managers of this organisation do a lot of telling but not much listening"*. The answer is more related to a company's overall rank than any other question in the survey. All 10 that scored highest on this question ended up in a top 20 position on the list.

The idea expanded – key findings

Somewhat worryingly, given that these are the best companies to work for and therefore by definition at the top of the pile, just 61% of the responses in the top 100 felt on balance that their bosses listened rather than told.

The link was so strong that firms with positive responses in this field score higher in all eight survey categories, leading to a higher final ranking. All of the 10 companies that achieved the best scores for bosses who listen and do not tell are in the top 20 overall and seven of those make the top 10 itself.

At 77.8% the average positive score for being listened to among the top 10 performers is nearly 13% above the average for the whole list. *If a company wanted to make a difference in its workplace the one single thing it could do is just start listening to people more.*

Listening makes a real difference to how staff feel about their company leadership. Where employees report lots of telling and not much listening bosses get just a 53.9% positive score compared with 81.3% at companies where staff feels they are listened to. So if you want to improve your leadership standing start to listen!

Drilling down further shows that among those reporting that bosses do a lot telling and not much listening, just 51.3% agree with the statement: "I have confidence in the leadership skills of the senior management team". This figure nearly doubles to 93.6% among staff who are listened to. If you want to improve confidence in your leadership skills start listening!

Interestingly, a close relationship also exists between being listened to and stress levels. Of the 10 questions that relate to stress levels this factor gets a 72.6% positive score compared with just 52.3% where comments fall on deaf ears. If people feel they are listened to they are much more likely to feel a sense of control and therefore feel less stressed.

Middle managers are hit the hardest. They return a 63.4% positive score on questions relating to well being. 66.7% and 66.5% are reported for team members and senior managers respectively. When we drill down into the telling v listening issue we find that it is those middle managers who strongly agree that 'senior managers do a lot of telling and not much listening' who are less content than colleagues above and below them. The more they disagree with the statement the greater their well being.

Evidence shows that where staff are listened to there is lower turnover and lower rates of absenteeism. Even in the best 'listening' companies 22.7% feel their organisation sometimes takes advantage. Compare this with the 63.9% whom feel taken advantage of if not listened to and the message is clearer still.

Even in the 100 Best Companies there is room for improvement. If you are not among the best the challenge is even greater.

The idea in practice – putting the idea to work

The practical implications? What one thing can I implement as a result of this research?

- Order a copy of the *DTI Report High Performance Work Practices: Linking Strategy and Skills to Performance Outcomes* (Tel: 0845 015 0010 Ref: URN 05/665). Assess your company – your activity – against each of the key themes in the report.
- Consult the *Information and Consultation Directive* via the DTI (www.dti.gov.uk/er/consultation/proposal.htm) which gives employees the right to be informed and consulted about what happens in their firm.
- Closer to home, bring the issues raised here down to a personal level. Rate *yourself* on a 1-7 scale (from Strongly Agree to Strongly Disagree) on the statement: *I do a lot of telling but not much listening.*

Now be brave and ask key members of your team to provide a rating.

What actions do your company/do you need to take to address the issues raised in this MRU?

3

Leading and Managing Performance

In our seminars and workshops on this core leadership topic there is one word that we try and imprint on each participant and that word is DIALOGUE. When we cut through all the sophistication and complexity of many performance management systems – and some systems are so complex there is no time left to actually manage performance – what we are left with is the need for three or four high quality 'dialogues' to take place each year between the manager and the employee. As long as this happens employees will feel that their performance is being actively managed.

Process versus Paper

But this is not so simple as it sounds. Because performance management is typically regarded as a system administered by the HR function, people tend to adopt a systems mindset. What this means is that managers and their staff focus on 'completing end-year appraisals' when in fact it is the real work that takes place during the year and which leads up to the end-year review that is the focus for managing performance. People end up supporting the system, doing what is administratively required, rather than actively engaging in a performance dialogue. It is the quality of the dialogue that will make the difference rather than the timely completion of the forms, however sophisticated these may be. Process is more important than paper.

Coaching

Clearly, in this schematic coaching is the engine that drives the performance management process. At each stage in the performance management cycle – goal setting –> interim reviews –> evaluation –> development planning – coaching has an important role to play as well as being an ongoing tool for managers to use. Giving employees the opportunity to work on the things they do best and coaching them to do these things better is probably the single best way to help an employee perform better.

Clarity and Empathy

As the diagram below shows, there are two simple concepts to get across when helping managers think about how they might conduct an affective dialogue. Like Jack Welch, ex-CEO of General Electric, we believe that management is one of the world's more simple professions. So we need to keep the performance dialogue simple. The two concepts are CLARITY and EMPATHY.* As long as employees are crystal clear about what performance means and feel that they have an effective relationship with their managers then the likelihood is that the performance dialogue will be meaningful to both parties.

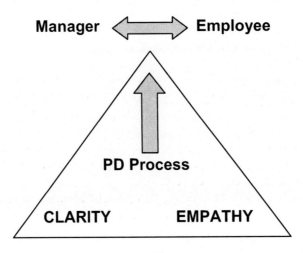

Clarity

Let us take CLARITY first. What exactly do we mean by 'clarity'? We mean, at least, three things.

First, we mean that there is an emphasis on facts and evidence rather than assumptions and supposition. Where there is a factual base, issues are more likely to be confronted constructively and robustly which in itself builds commitment because people are more likely to feel committed to something that has been properly discussed.

Secondly, we mean being clear about performance standards and expectations. There should be no confusion, no misinterpretation, no 'nods and winks' about what is expected. Both parties are on the same tramlines. What's more, not only is there clarity but the employee senses and feels that the manager actually believes that expectations and standards will be met.

Thirdly, we mean being clear about how well the employee is performing by providing regular feedback. A useful metaphor is to picture the employee as a guided missile. We want the missile to hit target. To hit target it needs a guidance system to keep it on trajectory. The guidance system is the feedback process. Regular, high quality feedback helps employees hit their targets.

So these three things help ensure CLARITY. They provide a hard business edge to the task of managing performance. But there is a softer side too, which runs in parallel.

Empathy

You cannot have an effective dialogue without an effective relationship and you cannot have an effective relationship without EMPATHY. Empathy requires at least three ingredients.

First, there has to be trust and trust takes time to build. The more regular the dialogue the greater the potential for building trust. As Charles Handy once said, trust is the cheapest form of control and managers like to feel in control.

To build trust there needs to be open and honest communications. No matter how many times this is said people still find it difficult to tell the truth simply and directly. Some cultures, in our experience, are better at this than others (for example, the Dutch and Belgian).

Thirdly, for empathy to be felt, the employee needs to feel that someone out there actually cares and is there to help. It is the manager's job to provide whatever support and guidance may be required. As the Americans tend to say, 'managers need to go and bat for their employees.'

So these three things help to ensure EMPATHY which provides a softer people edge to the performance dialogue. So remember the simple formula:

Effective Performance Dialogue = f(Clarity + Empathy)

Characteristics of a Performance Management Process

An effective performance dialogue is more likely to take place where the wider performance management process possesses three characteristics.

First, it should be regarded as joint problem-solving process. That is to say, the manager and employee come together as equals to address performance-related issues on the basis of shared information.

Secondly, the performance management process should be an empowering rather than a judgmental process. People should feel more not less free to figure out how they might achieve their goals and deliver on their commitments. People should feel good about participating in the process.

Thirdly, the performance management process should be regarded as both an emotional and intellectual process. Employees need to be emotionally committed to their goals and tasks (the 'what') which is why they must be fully discussed and agreed rather than merely accepted. They also need to be smart and innovative about achieving these – to use their talents in accomplishing tough goals (the 'how'). Engage people's hearts determining their goals (the 'what'). Engage their brains in developing plans to achieve the goals (the 'how'). The elegance of a performance management process lies in bringing together effectively both the 'what' and the 'how'.

Figure 5 below summarises the key features outlined in this chapter:

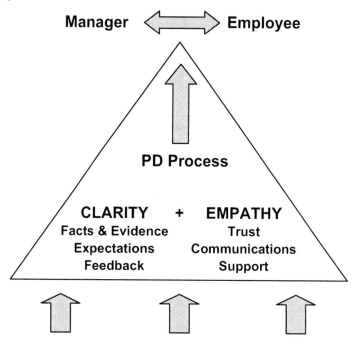

Figure 5:Performance Dialogue

The readings that follow focus primarily on what is required to achieve high performance. But they also embrace two contextual readings which underscore the importance of meaning at work and the features that are most likely to stop people feeling miserable in the jobs they have. Leading and managing performance is a key component of execution, one of the three elements that comprise our effective organisational leadership framework outlined in Chapter 2.

*The author credits his colleague Phil Lowe for this concept.

READING 9

The high performance organisation

Harvard Business Review Collection

The focus of **Reading 9** is the *high performance organisation* and the source is 194 pages of the July-August 2005 'double issue' of the *Harvard Business Review*.

For a journal with a reputation for helping organisations improve, it would be disappointing not to find a sizeable handful of useable nuggets for the practising manager.

With less than 30% of the US workforce described as 'energised ' or 'committed' something clearly needs to be injected into the bloodstream of corporate America if not the rest of the world.

The idea in brief – the 'core' idea

Many companies claim to be (or certainly want to be) high performance organisations (HPOs in the jargon). The problem lies in defining them. A 20-year look at the findings of ten top research teams provides no quick answers as far as the academics are concerned.

Whilst in reality the real thing is rare, it is immediately recognisable on sight ('we know it when we see it'). In practical terms we are talking about that elite circle of companies where exceptional performance is an everyday occurrence. Contemporary (and we emphasise the word contemporary) examples probably include Toyota, General Electric and Dell to name but a few.

Naming is not the same as explaining however, which is the purpose of this MRU. By distilling common themes and patterns from the myriad of data that comprise the HBR edition used as source material we hope to shed some practical light on some of the key factors shared by (at least today's) organisational performers.

The idea expanded – key findings

The eclectic collection of ideas and (research) findings documented in the edition under review break down into four overlapping arenas, none of which will come as a surprise to regular readers of the management literature. Each arena comprises issues relating to:

- **Leadership** – both business and personal.
- **Teams** – both leading them and working in them.
- **Learning** – critically, learning from experience.
- **Organisation design** – particularly creativity.

To which we would add two more (with apologies to HBR). First, recognition that performance like success feeds on itself. Secondly, that success can breed active inertia. Which probably explains why over 20 years that list of high performance organisations just keeps on changing.

So what are the messages, the takeaways for each of these high performance arenas?

Leadership

- Business leadership – huge focus on execution. Bearing in mind on average companies deliver 63% of the financial performance their strategies promise some useful rules to help turn strategy into performance are:

  - Keep it simple – make it concrete – state what the company will and won't do.
  - Debate assumptions not forecasts.
  - Use a rigorous analytic framework.
  - Discuss resource deployments early.
  - Ruthlessly identify priorities.
  - Continually monitor performance.
  - Reward and develop execution capabilities.

- Personal leadership – **draw on one's own values and capabilities** rather than imitating others. Four transforming questions to ask yourself:

- Am I truly results orientated? Will I leave my traditional comfort zone to make things happen?
- Am I internally directed? Do I behave in a way that reflects my values or do "I bend with the wind?"
- Am I "other" focused? Do I put the collective good beyond my own immediate needs?
- Am I externally open? Am I receptive to outside stimuli and the need for change?

If you answer an unequivocal 'yes' to these questions you are probably leading in the truest sense.

Teams:

- **Get the basics right** – the size, the structure, the selection, the processes. Be prepared to 'lose' non-deliverers. Avoid becoming a pseudo-team.
- **Take time to build shared commitment** – shared commitment comes from a shared purpose and this doesn't happen overnight. With shared purpose comes shared goals and shared accountability.
- **Focus on team performance not team building** – avoid the warm bath syndrome ('polite teams produce polite results'). Introduce edge. Raise (to an extent) the stress level.
- **Manage the employee/customer interface** – recognise that employee engagement correlates with customer engagement. Focus on the emotional aspects. Teams that do this outperform their peers by 26% in gross margins and 85% in sales growth.
- **Be prepared to break the rules** – teams convened for very special purposes have frenetic rhythm, discernible energy and impassioned dialogue. Don't assume the conventional rules of collaboration always apply. The team leader may have to herd cats.

We would also add that a high performance team is more likely to flourish where there is both a compelling business and a compelling people need. So often, one or the other is present, but not both. Back to the pseudo-team.

Learning

The 'big idea' here is **AAR (After Action Review)** – the process of extracting lessons from an event or project so as to apply them to others. This is different from 'learning after the event' or conducting a 'post-mortem' or carrying out a 'performance review'.

The key to AAR is that the lessons have not been learned *until they have been successfully applied and validated.* Four vital rules apply:

- The lessons learned must benefit those that extract them.
- The process must start at the beginning not the end.
- The lessons must link to future actions.
- Leaders must hold everyone accountable for learning – including themselves.

Organisation Design

Three key factors drive organisation design for high performance:

- **Designing high performance jobs** by building in four 'spans' – control (resources), accountability (measures), influence (interaction) and support (help). Adjust the settings for the situation. For example, for control the settings will be narrower for a Wal-Mart store manager than for a corporate merchandising manager.

- **Creating vibrant human networks** by specifying rules for effective collaboration – rules about how individuals and groups communicate and work together to achieve a common goal. In the tea sipping, disciplined, clean-cut world of Toyota they pride themselves on 'taking averagely talented people and making them work as spectacular teams'. They do it by:
  - Using simple, pervasive technology.
  - Keeping work visible (seeing everyone's real work).
  - Building communities of trust.
  - Thinking modularly not linearly.
  - Encouraging teaming (for example, by dismantling individual performance metrics).

- **Harnessing the creative energy of all the stakeholders by:**
  - Keeping employees intellectually engaged and removing distractions.
  - Making managers responsible for sparking creativity ('we're all creative').
  - Engaging customers as creative partners (making customers' voices as loud and clear and unambiguous as the share price).

The SAS Institute, which predictably makes the Fortune 100 best companies to work for each year and has 28 straight years of revenue growth recognises that 95% of its assets drive out the door each evening. The leader's job is the get them back each morning. (Apply the elevator test: observe the employees waiting for the elevator in the morning – are they rushing in late – or rushing out early? Do they whistle to work? Do they look as though they work in a creative environment?). Back to the employee – customer interface.

To quote Gary Hamel the strategy guru: "We want hierarchies of imagination not hierarchies of experience".

The idea in practice – putting the idea to work
The practical implications? What one thing can I implement a result of this research?

As OED's focus is leaders *in* organisations rather than leaders *of* organisations our challenge is to apply the findings here to your own work unit.
On a scale of 1-10 to what extent are you truly leading a high performance work unit?

If you are:
Take purposeful action to avoid 'active inertia'. This means:

- Ensuring your 'strategic lens' does not become rigid and blind your peripheral vision (remember National Westminster Bank?)
- Questioning every single process to make sure they are not just

comfortable habits that could block change (remember Compaq?)

- Checking that your tangible and intangible resources remain difficult to replicate by competitors (remember large airlines and the entry of the low cost airlines?)
- Preventing your external relationships turning into shackles that limit flexibility (remember Daewoo?)
- Not letting values harden into outdated dogmas (remember Laura Ashley?)

If you are not:

Simply pick *one idea* from the above. One you think you can do something with. One that will give you the greatest bang for the buck. Get your team around it, flawlessly execute it, learn the lessons and figure out how you can be more creative next time round.

After all, that's what being a high performance organisation is all about.

READING 10

Leading extraordinary performance

Kim Cameron & Marc Lavine

In 1995 the US Department of Energy faced the decision to close the Rocky Flats nuclear weapons production facility. No clean up or closure of such a site had ever occurred anywhere in the world so there was no precedent and no known operating procedures. The estimate of closure and clean up: 70 years and $36 billion – to be completed in 2065. By 10 October 2005 – 60 years early – the task was completed $30 billion under budget, 13 times cleaner than required and 200 technological innovations en route. Safety came in at twice as good as the industry average while unions worked themselves out of a job and former adversaries and antagonists became advocates and supporters. The story is told in *Making the Impossible Possible – Leading Extraordinary Performance* by Kim Cameron & Marc Lavine, which illustrates leaders applying an abundance approach to change.

(This Reading summarises the approach drawing on research conducted primarily by Kim Cameron at the Michigan Ross School of Business (www. bus.umich.edu) and published with permission)

The idea in brief – the 'core' idea

The abundance approach to change contrasts directly with what most of us recognise as the traditional problem solving approach:

Problem Solving Approach

- Define the problem.
- Identify symptoms and root causes.
- Generate options that address issues and evaluate.
- Implement preferred solutions.

Abundance Approach

- Identify peak performance by re-counting spectacular experiences.
- Explain past successes by identifying enablers.
- Identify what should be continued to create sustainability.
- Design interventions that create ideal futures.

Whereas the problem solving approach rests on the assumption that the job is to **overcome major problems and obstacles** the abundance approach adopts the mindset that that the job is **to embrace and enable people's highest potential**.

By focusing on abundance gaps (positive deviance from normal) rather than deficit gaps (negative deviance from normal) it is possible to create what the authors call the *heliotropic effect* at the centre of which lies the capability to produce **positive energies**.

The idea expanded – key findings

A **systematic bias** exists in people that shows that the occurrence of negative factors are more powerful than positive factors – in short, **'bad is stronger than good'** (think television News).

People seem to be more affected by one traumatic/negative event than by one positive/happy event. They seem to be more affected emotionally from a single piece of negative feedback than from a single piece of positive feedback. Why?

Evolutionary theory suggests that if people ignore negative – or threatening – feedback it could cost them their lives. If they ignore positive feedback it causes them regret.

So it's not surprising that negative phenomena get more attention than positive phenomena. It takes a very conscious effort to focus on abundance, which in contrast leverages positive energisers.

Those who positively energise others are more likely to be higher performers. Position in the *energy network* is four times the predictor of performance compared to position in *informational* networks.

Positive energisers also tend to enhance the work of others.

People who interact with or are connected to energisers tend to perform better.

High performing firms have three times as many positive energising networks than low performing firms.

Based on research after downsizing across 16 industries a statistically significant relationship was found to exist between both objective (e.g. financial, quality) and perceived (e.g. employee engagement, turnover) performance ($p < .01$) and practices related to the abundance approach.

Conclusion: **By engaging in such practices organisational effectiveness can be significantly improved.**

The idea in practice – putting the idea to work

The practical implications? What one thing can I implement as a result of this research?

Conduct your own mini-survey:
- Who in *your* networks are positive energisers (name them)?
- Are they in the majority or the minority?
- What happens to *your* energy when you interact with them?
- What is *your* emotional reaction to them?
- What is the impact on *your* relationship with them?
- What do they *do differently* from others in your networks?
- How might *you* leverage this to become a positive energiser and create extraordinary performance in your organisation?

READING 11

The seven keys to high performance

Corporate Leadership Council

Research reveals countless definitions of *the high performance organisation*. Although there is some agreement between researchers on the ideals of the HPO few seem to agree on the specific characteristics that support and operationalise these ideals.

Research conducted by the Corporate Leadership Council* (www.corporateleadershipcouncil.com) unpacks this complex theme to identify quantitatively the effectiveness of performance management strategies. It is a first-class piece of empirical research based on survey results from 19,000 respondents from 34 companies, seven industry sectors and 29 countries. The practical implications for individual managers are clear and compelling.

Reading 11 summarises the key findings of this research and highlights the key practices leaders and managers can engage in which the research shows will achieve performance improvement of at least 25%.

The idea in brief – the 'core' idea

The basic premise of the research is that the inability of performance management to guarantee performance improvement has two root causes:

1. Not knowing *what* matters most to individual performance
2. Not knowing *how* to leverage individual performance to improve results.

The research investigated seven categories of potential performance drivers (see headings below). Within each of these the direct and indirect impact on employee performance was tested. Some factors

81

measurably improved *high-performance attitudes* (e.g. job satisfaction, organisational commitment) which in turn improved *employee performance*. Other factors had a direct impact on *individual performance*. When combined, the shift in performance on a number of factors was considerable.

Together, these factors in rank-order of their impact on individual performance provide a road map for effective performance management for the practising manager.

The idea expanded – key findings

The Performance Management System – the singular power of clarity

Overall, the content or 'nuts and bolts' of performance reviews (e.g. the number and type of reviews) have a much lower impact than *employee understanding of the standards on which they are evaluated*.

The average impact of employee understanding of performance standards according to the research is about seven times that of most of the other characteristics of performance management systems.

A 36% increase in employee performance is predicted when attitudinal changes are combined with a positive direct impact of 31.4%.

Performance Culture – the freedom to take risks, communicate and be flexible

The cultural trait with the largest impact on employee performance is *risk taking* – the extent to which an organisation encourages high-risk, high-return ideas and investments (internal communications and organisational flexibility come next).

Attitudinal changes combined with a positive direct impact are predicted to drive a 39% increase in employee performance (34% and 23% for internal communication and organisational flexibility respectively).

Manager-Employee Interaction – solutions enabler

The manager behaviour that drives the biggest improvement is *helping employees find solutions to problems at work.* Managers also play a key role in attaining necessary resources or solutions, managing projects and clearly communicating expectations.

Attitudinal changes combined with a positive direct impact are predicted to drive a 24% increase in employee performance (in comparison, recognising and rewarding achievement drive a 4% improvement).

Formal Review – the delicate balance between praise and criticism

Emphasising performance strengths drives a 36% improvement in performance, almost 60% higher than performance weaknesses, which can cause a 29% decline in employee performance.

Interestingly, focusing on the positive does more for employee performance than specific suggestions for doing the job better, emphasis on skills and behaviours needed for the future or emphasis on long-term career prospects within the organisation.

Informal Feedback – the primacy of fairness and accuracy

Fair and accurate informal feedback has a positive indirect effect on employee performance. In addition, it has a positive direct impact of 34%.

Taken together, these indirect and direct effects of fair and accurate informal feedback improve employee performance by 40%.

In addition, how much employees think their manager knows about their level of performance and informal feedback that helps employees do their job better have both a positive indirect and direct impact on performance, driving an overall improvement in employee performance levels of 30% and 26% respectively.

Day-to-Day Work – connection over rewards

As a category, *personal connection* is most important with an average impact of 11% on employee performance.

In practical terms this means ensuring that employees understand how to successfully complete their work, followed by ensuring that they personally enjoy their work, have influence in selecting projects and find their work challenging.

Ensuring that employees understand how to successfully complete their work drives key employee attitudes and has a positive direct effect. **Together, they account for a 13% improvement in employee performance.**

(In contrast, the impact of financial incentives is greater on attraction and retention than it is on performance, driving down retention by almost 20% but increasing employee performance by just 2%).

Job Opportunities – high profile, good fit and new skills

Overall, *on-the-job development performance levers* have the greatest impact on performance, followed by functional training (in particular IT training) and then general training.

The single biggest improvement in employee performance that can be had from on-the-job development is in *giving employees the opportunity to work on the things they do best.*

When the direct effect on employee performance of 25% is combined with the indirect effect through attitudinal improvement, performance levels rise by almost 30%.

Following that, the biggest performance levers are working for a strong executive team with a performance impact of 26%.

* Published with permission from the Corporate Executive Board of the Corporate Leadership Council (CCL)

The idea in practice – putting the idea to work

The practical implications? What one thing can I implement as a result of this research?

The chart below lists the *A-level performance drivers* in order of their impact on performance. These nine factors drive the largest improvements in employee performance and provide a practical road map for effective performance management.

While no one 'category' drives performance each of the items listed is predicted to increase individual performance by 25% or more.

1. Fairness and accuracy of informal feedback **(39%)**
2. Risk taking **(39%)**
3. Emphasis (in formal review) on performance strengths **(36%)**
4. Employee understanding of performance standards **(36%)**
5. Internal communication – between peers and between managers and employees **(34%)**
6. Manager knowledgeable about performance **(30%)**
7. Opportunity to work on things the employee does best **(29%)**
8. Feedback that helps employees do their jobs better **(26%)**
9. Opportunity to work for a strong executive team **(26%)**

So how do YOU stack up in terms of managing your employees' performance?

READING 12

The seven deadly sins of performance management

Michael Hammer

At a privately held logistics company senior executives were dissatisfied with the performance measurement system despite considerable success in the marketplace. By identifying a key operating metric and improving the business processes that supported it they managed to increase 'perfect orders' from its initial value of 6% to nearly 80%. As a result, operating costs were dramatically reduced, customer satisfaction increased and margins enhanced. One of many examples cited in the Spring 2007 edition of the *Sloan Management Review* (see Special Report: Measuring to Manage – The 7 Deadly Sins of Performance Measurement by Michael Hammer). This Reading summarises the key points in the article.

The idea in brief – the 'core' idea

Operational performance measurement is not one of the sexy fads that dominate the business press. At least not since the days when virtually every company was engaged in some form of business process re-engineering. However, despite the relatively little attention it gets, identifying and using an **effective set of metrics** is fundamental to good performance management and achievement of strategic goals.

In the article, Hammer outlines the recurring mistakes that impede the relevance and usefulness of operating measures. He refers to these as the *seven deadly sins of performance management*: Sins that present grave dangers to the prospects for superior business performance.

The idea expanded – key findings

Sin Number 1: Vanity

One of the most widespread mistakes in performance measurement is to use measures that will **make the organisation, its people and especially its managers look good**. "Nobody wants a metric that they don't score 95 on".

This is particularly the case since bonuses and other rewards are usually tied to results measured in terms of performance measures.

Sin Number 2: Provincialism

This is the sin of letting **organisational boundaries and concerns** dictate performance metrics. While on the surface it seems natural for a functional department (for example, HR) to be measured on its own performance in reality measuring narrowly leads to sub-optimisation.

For instance, in a financial institution it may be the job of the sales team to generate more deals while the job of the credit department is to manage risk. Clearly, the two are in conflict and a lot of management's emotional energy can go into resolving the conflict which is exacerbated when people in each department are evaluated on metrics designed only for their department rather than for a higher order goal that benefits the total business.

Sin Number 3: Narcissism

This is the unpardonable offence of **measuring from one's own point of view** rather than from the customer's perspective.

For example, a retailer might achieve a 98% score by measuring whether goods-in-stores match stock-on-hand levels specified in the merchandising plan when in fact what is critical is measuring goods-in-store with what customers actually want to buy which may, of course, be lower.

Sin Number 4: Laziness

Assuming one knows what is important to measure **without giving it adequate thought or effort**. For example, a manufacturer measured many aspects of its order processing operation but not the critical (to customers) issue of how long it took from the time the customer gave the order to the time the company confirmed the order and provided a delivery date – simply because it never thought of asking customers what was important to them.

Sin Number 5: Pettiness

Too often, a business measures only **a small part of what matters**. For instance, a telecommunications company rejected a proposal to have customers perform their own repairs as this would require putting spare parts at customer premises that would drive up inventory. It lost sight of a key metric for the company – *total* cost of maintenance.

Sin Number 6: Inanity

Many companies seem to implement metrics without giving any thought to the **consequences of these metrics on human behaviour** and ultimately on business performance. People in organisations will always seek to improve a metric they are told is important, especially if they are compensated for it.

For example, a fast-food chain wanted to improve financial performance by reducing waste. They did this by telling staff not to cook chicken until it was ordered. This had the effect of turning a fast-food chain into a slow-food chain. Waste did decline but so did sales.

Sin Number 7: Frivolity

The most serious sin of all. It is manifested by **arguing about metrics instead of taking them to heart, by finding excuses for poor performance rather than root causes and by looking for ways to pass the blame.** While the other errors are sins of the intellect this is a sin of character and organisation culture.

These seven categories overlap and are related. **A business that commits these sins will find itself unable to use its metrics to drive improvements in operating performance.** As the old adage goes "that which is measured gets done". But if you are measuring the wrong thing, making it better will simply make more important things worse. A serious commitment to performance improvement demands an equally serious commitment to designing and using effective operational metrics.

* Adapted excerpts from The Seven Deadly Sins of Performance Management by Michael Hammer, MIT Sloan Management Review (Spring 2007) by permission of publisher. © 2007 by Massachusetts Institute of Technology. All rights reserved.

The idea in practice – putting the idea to work

The practical implications? What one thing can I implement as a result of this research?

The four steps to redemption:

1. **Select the right things to measure**, those aspects of business performance that are both *controllable* and *important to success*:

   - Decide what to measure by emphasising *end-to-end processes* and determining *business drivers* in terms of these processes.

2. **Measure these things in the right ways** by balancing the following:

   - Precision and accuracy – ensuring the metric is well-defined and measures what you want to measure.
   - Overhead – avoiding over-complexity.
   - Robustness – avoiding sub-optimisation, undesired behaviours and manipulation (maybe through using multiple rather than single metrics).

3. **Embed the metrics in a disciplined process** by:

   - Assigning accountability for the metric to one or more

individuals (including both process owners and functional managers involved in the process).

- Ensuring a target level for each metric and 'managing the gap' between desired and actual (gap analysis usually = process design flaw and/or execution flaw).

4. **Create a measurement-friendly culture** by:

- Discouraging 'seat-of-the-pants' management style.
- Engaging the most senior leaders in role modelling ("Setting an example is not the main means of influencing others. It is the only means". Albert Einstein) to demonstrate commitment.
- Using reward to reinforce the use of the right metrics.
- Incorporating them into management development and training programmes.
- Constantly articulating them.

When *all* these are used the results, claim the author, can be measurably impressive.

Closing thought

The fundamental point of measurement is not to measure. It is to enable performance improvement. Therefore, it must be an integral part of any company's performance management process. How many of us can put our hands on our hearts and say that the metrics we deploy measure the right things, in the right way, in the right kind of environment?

READING 13

Managing for high performance

Mckinsey Research

Reading 13 distils the findings from research by McKinsey based on 115,000 responses from more than 230 organisations around the world. They show that strong organisational performance is more likely to result from **a combination of three or four carefully selected management practices than by isolated interventions, however fashionable and guru-driven they may be.**

Executives should therefore eschew simplistic organisational solutions: when applied in isolation popular techniques such as management incentives and key performance indicators (KPIs) were found to be strikingly ineffective. High performing organisations are more likely to have a basic proficiency in all of the 34 practices with a conspicuous weakness in any of them likely to drag down the overall result.

The idea in brief – the 'core' idea

While organisations don't need superior abilities in all of the practices and a failure to achieve basic competence in any of them drags down the performance of the whole some choices are clearly superior.

One combination of practices increases the overall effectiveness of organisations more than others do. Senior executives must provide ACCOUNTABILITY, DIRECTION and A PERFORMANCE CULTURE.

Applied in combination, these three practices produce much more dramatic results because they have a *mutually reinforcing dynamic* – i.e. increasing the amount of effort behind any one practice increases the likelihood of achieving not only its target outcome but also the other target outcomes, thus making organisations more effective overall.

For most people the way these three practices – clear roles, an inspiring vision and an open and trusting culture – interact to create complementarities is intuitively clear. **Employees perform well when they are working towards a future that attracts them, know when they can operate freely and are encouraged to improve constantly.**

Companies in the research that applied the base case were found to outperform others in terms of revenues and margins. The link between organisational effectiveness and financial performance was demonstrated.

The idea expanded – key findings

Accountability

Leaders need to make people feel ACCOUNTABLE. In practical terms that means **feeling responsible for the results of the business.** Companies seeking to improve in this area are much more likely to succeed if they concentrate on giving employees CLEAR ROLES.

Direction

Executives who set BROAD STRETCHING ASPIRATIONS that are meaningful to their employees have a better chance of achieving the outcome they want than do executives who resort to conventional, dominant or top-down leadership.

A performance culture

The research offers statistical evidence that the best way to promote high-performance behaviour in organisations is to emphasise OPENNESS and TRUST among employees.

Conclusion

The base case outlined was found to be equally successful in manufacturing, financial and pharmaceutical companies. The data did not tell us that the base case is less effective in any particular context. A company's performance is much more likely to be improved by a combination of complementary practices – especially those that provide for **clear accountability**, help set **goals and priorities** and encourage **a high performing culture** through openness and trust.

The idea in practice – putting the idea to work

Take a long, hard look at the area for which you are responsible. Answer the following for *yourself*:

On a scale of 1-5 to what extent do *you* feel:

1. Responsible for the area *you* manage?
2. That you have a clear direction?
3. There is openness and trust in the wider organisation of which you are a part?

Now answer the same questions again but for the people **you** manage rather than for you.

If you don't know the answers, maybe it's time to ask them.

READING 14

Coaching with edge: thoughts from a business coach

Dr Fred Cannon

My thoughts are those of a business coach. Which means that the lessons from experience I want to share are based primarily on coaching business leaders at different levels in different types of organisation.

More often than not the focus is on behavioural change because this is what achievement-orientated executives tend to struggle with most. They are bound to because it is highly likely they have been successful – i.e. reached a senior position, because they have the intelligence, business acumen and drive to succeed. Being behaviourally competent without these commercial attributes would have done little for their careers and even less for their bank balances.

Most readers will be familiar with the traditional skills of coaching and the need to be concrete and precise in working through with the client the what's, when's and how's if development goals are to be committed to and achieved. I believe the greater challenge is to balance the required level of support and challenge in the coaching process. **Too often, in my experience, coaches are apt to slip into over-supportive mode because that is their natural comfort zone and personal value set.** While this makes for a comfortable, touchy-feely relationship, senior level executives are unlikely to change if all they experience is a warm bath. Discomfort is an inevitable part of the personal change process and it is the coach's job to provide it.

I call this brand of coaching 'coaching with edge'.

Significant change in behaviour requires a significant change in mental maps – the way executives have learnt to see the world around them. Changing a person's mental map requires some kind of catalytic event, experience or insight otherwise it will be an intellectual rather than an emotional exercise. For such insights to be useful and to be potent enough to form the basis for new habits they need to be generated from within, not served up by the coach or anyone else on a plate. **The essence of 'coaching with edge' is to help the person being coached to experience truly meaningful insights.** This is partly to do with how the person is coached but also a lot to do with the steps in the journey that precede this. As with all successful journeys, the key is careful, detailed preparation – having the patience and taking the time to build the foundations and chart the course that will ensure the client reaches the end of the journey.

The idea in brief – the 'core' idea

So where is the best place to start? The best place to start is with what matters most to the business leader and generally that is the business for which the leader is responsible. Let me be specific. **The only reason the person is being coached is because that will help the individual contribute more to the business.** There is no other reason.

The idea expanded – key findings

So the place to start is to agree with the individual what the overarching goal for the business is. Expressing in one, focused sentence where the leader wants the business to be is the first step in the coaching journey. Get this wrong or accept a fudgy outcome and progress will not be made.

Once there is agreement about the overarching business goal it is time to talk about performance because if there is one thing senior executives understand it is performance. The question to be answered at this stage is very straightforward: **'What are the two or three strategic areas of competence that will have the greatest potential impact on achieving the overarching business goal?'** For example, the overarching business goal might be: 'increase European revenues to 25% of global revenues in three years' and the related areas of strategic competence: 'strategic thinking', 'innovative business development' and 'team leadership'. By applying the 'if ' test – i.e. 'if I am fully competent in these areas will I deliver the business goal?' the coach can check the relevance of what has been agreed.

Notice that at this stage we are keeping the thinking relatively high level. We do not zoom in (yet) on a small set of critical leader behaviours – this comes later. **All we do is identify what the executive must excel at if s/he is to deliver the overarching business goal.** Clearly, some probing questions will unpack each of the critical areas but it is important not to let this go too far at this early stage. While defined areas of competence – for example, those used in the company's 360-degree process – may be relevant, it is best to use these as a backdrop and get the client to think through from first principles using his or her own language. That way, ownership lies with the individual rather than the HR department.

Now it's time to go external. We need to know whom the core stakeholders are and what they think to ensure that we get a balanced, external perspective on the leader's current effectiveness. So first we agree with the executive (and his/her manager) who the stakeholders are and why. Then, face-to face interviews are conducted rather than using a survey tool because the process needs to be interactive.

People simply do not respond in the same way using written responses, however sophisticated the tool.

In the spirit of ownership, the client rather than the coach communicates with the stakeholders, explains the purpose of the interviews and sets everything up.

During the interview the coach first checks out the areas of competence already identified by the business leader. There needs to be alignment between the views of the executive and those of the stakeholders. If this is not the case then further discussion with the client is required. Once there is alignment the probing starts in order to identify two or three critical behaviours in each area of competence. At this stage, it's quite useful to be quantitative. For example, on a scale of 1-10 how important is that behaviour to the leader's role? On the same scale, how effective is the executive in practising these behaviours? By starting to build a matrix of data comprising levels/groups of stakeholders and behaviours, patterns start to emerge which will feed the development goals to be agreed with the client during the coaching sessions that follow. The 'zooming in' process has begun.

We have now reached the point in the journey where it is time to share the data collected with the client. While there are differing viewpoints about whether it is best to do this verbally or in the form of a written report, my own view favours both. That is, prepare the data in the form of a feedback report (including the results of any psychometrics which will provide a continuing point of reference during the coaching process and help the coach and client understand each other's styles) because business executives are used to and expect hard data to be presented professionally. They would not expect a market research study to be presented verbally. However, I do recommend that the feedback is presented verbally to ensure that both the messages and the reactions can be managed. The executive can then digest the feedback report in the period before the next meeting takes place in readiness for moving into the developmental phase of the coaching process.

In 'coaching with edge' there are five questions the coach needs answers to by the end of the feedback sharing session. They are:

Q1 Do you recognise and accept the feedback outlined in this report?
Yes or no?

Q2 Are you able (with help) to change?
Yes or no?

Q3 Do you want to (in a serious and sustained rather than cosmetic way)?
Yes or no?

Q4 Why? Be specific.

Q5 Are you willing to do whatever it takes (for example: including allowing me to help you; talking openly about your commitment to change)?
Yes or no?

This is the walk-away point.

If following serious discussion the executive is unable to answer an authentic 'yes' to each of these five questions then there is a strong case for terminating the coaching process. There is no point in investing time, money and skills on someone who only wants to go through the motions. Or as a colleague of mine once put it: "To have a bath without getting wet."

At this stage, most coaches would probably start coaching by setting developmental goals from the feedback data. I prefer a slightly different route for two important reasons. First, stakeholders need to know that the person being coached is fully committed to personal change, that **something is going to happen.** Secondly, the client needs to be sure that s/he has fully understood the feedback that has been collated. **This is best achieved by sharing top-line feedback directly with stakeholder groups** (for example, a group of peers, a group of direct reports etc.). The executive takes responsibility for this process with the coach providing professional support.

It is critical to get this process right. The aim is not to identify 'who said what' or to duplicate the feedback that has already been given. Rather, it provides the opportunity for the executive to play back, check understanding and explore the messages that have emerged from the feedback process. It may also be appropriate for people to make suggestions to the executive about what s/he might do differently going forward. (This 'feedforward' process helps to shift the focus from past to future behaviours). These suggestions can then be accessed during the coaching sessions. Managing these feedback meetings is a skilled process to ensure that integrity is not breached and that further added-value is gained from people who have already given their time in one-to-one interviews. The coach's job is to structure the meetings and keep a light hand on the tiller throughout the proceedings.

Now we are ready to move into the more familiar developmental phase of coaching (although much of the above requires well-developed coaching skills). In the same way as 80% of a sale lies in preparation, so the quality of the groundwork laid out above will impact on the success of the coaching. Together, the client and the coach revisit the feedback data, including the outputs of the feedback meetings described above. The shared task is first, to agree the coaching goal – i.e. where the client will be at the end of the coaching programme and secondly, the priority behaviours that will deliver the goal. What we are looking for here is the smallest number of behaviours with the maximum impact around which coaching will be focused over something like a six-month period. With clarity about what needs to change the shared effort can focus on the all-important how's.

When the coaching sessions have been completed we are ready for the final step in the journey. The client, the stakeholders and the coach will want to know **'has it worked?'** It therefore makes sense to contact the original interviewees to ascertain the degree of progress made. I suggest keeping this very simple. Via email or telephone, a mini-item questionnaire that allows respondents to quantify the amount of change observed is all that is required. The results of this can then be integrated into a summary coaching session when it is also useful to communicate, simply but powerfully, the core message that will inspire and help the executive to sustain future efforts. Follow-up, routine coaching may then continue to help ensure that hard-earned insights remain hardwired through repeated attention and focus.

The idea in practice – putting the idea to work

1. Make a list of potential coaching candidates in your area of responsibility.

2. Rate each one on a 1-5 scale for a) current effectiveness b) potential impact on the business c) future potential – and then rank the candidates (low effectiveness, high impact on business and high potential puts a candidate at the top).

3. Establish your budget and to ensure you do not spread it too thinly assume 15k per candidate. If this means coaching one candidate so be it. This is a high investment strategy.

This article first appeared in *Coach & Mentor* (Spring 2007), The Journal of the Oxford School of Coaching & Mentoring. Adapted and published with permission.

READING 15

The three signs of a miserable job

Patrick Lencioni

This **Reading** summarises the latest book by the same author as *The Five Dysfunctions of a Team* (see **Reading 21**), Patrick Lencioni: *The Three Signs of a Miserable Job* (Jossey Bass).*

As usual, the read is easy and the messages clear, notwithstanding Lucy Kellaway's comments in the *Financial Times* (12 November 2007).

The idea in brief – the 'core' idea

A miserable job is not the same as a bad one.

Everyone knows what a miserable job is and they are found everywhere. It's the one people dread going to and can't wait to leave. It's the one that saps your energy and makes you more cynical at the end of the day than you were at the start.

But being miserable has little to do with the work itself. **Three underlying factors will make a job miserable and they apply to virtually all jobs regardless of the nature of the work being done.** These three factors may seem obvious yet according to Lencioni they remain largely unaddressed in most organisations.

The idea expanded – key findings

So what are these three obvious factors that have the potential to make the lives of our employees miserable?

Anonymity

People cannot be fulfilled in their work if they are not known. All human beings need to be understood and appreciated for their

101

unique qualities by someone in a position of authority. People who see themselves as invisible, generic or anonymous cannot love their jobs, no matter what they are doing.

Irrelevance

Everyone needs to know that his or her job matters – to someone. **Without seeing a connection between the work and the satisfaction of another (or others) an employee simply will not find lasting fulfilment.** The work needs to matter to someone.

Measurement

Employees need to be able to gauge their progress and level of contribution for *themselves*. They cannot be fulfilled in their work if their success depends on the opinions of another person. Without tangible means for assessing success or failure, motivation will deteriorate as people feel they are unable to control their own fate.

What simple practices can a manager engage in to address these three causes of misery?

* The Three Signs of a Miserable Job, Patrick Lencioni © Patrick Lencioni, 2007. Reproduced with permission of John Wiley & Sons Inc.

The idea in practice – putting the idea to work

The practical implications? What one thing can I implement as a result of this research?

Anonymity

The most effective way to remove any sense of anonymity from employees' situations at work is to **get to know them**.

Take time to sit down with each of them and ask them what's going on in their lives. In short, take a **genuine** interest (no faking – it doesn't work).

To manage another human being effectively requires some degree of **empathy and curiosity** about why that person gets out of bed each morning.

Taking a personal interest is not something to be ticked off the list. It needs to be **reinforced, ongoing and demonstrated repeatedly**.

Most people get out of bed to live their lives and their work is one part of their lives. **People want to be managed as people rather than mere employees.**

Irrelevance

Human beings **need to be needed** and they need to be reminded of this pretty much every day.

Being needed implies **having an impact on the lives of others**. When people believe they have no impact at all they begin to die emotionally. Managers therefore need to help employees answer two questions:

1. *Who am I helping?*

For some it will be external or internal customers, or perhaps another department or team member. For the CEO it may be the executive team.

But for many it will be the boss. So sometimes, **managers must help employees understand that their work impacts on them.**

2. *How?*

Managers need to help employees figure out exactly how they are helping? What is the real outcome of the tasks they perform?

Managers need to be able to see beyond what their employees are doing and help them understand who they are helping and how they are making a difference.

(Why, for example, is it that employees at SW Airlines are doing largely the same job as employees at other airlines but there are fewer miserable jobs there?)

In short, managers help employees to see why their work matters to someone.

Immeasurement

Immeasurement (not in the dictionary) is an employee's **lack of a clear means of assessing her or his progress or success on the job** which leads to ambiguity and a feeling of dependence on a manager to judge the employee's achievements.

Great employees don't want their success to depend on the subjective views of others. They do not want the politicking and posturing that goes with this. **Great employees want measurables so that they can get an intrinsic sense of accomplishment.** (*Ed: It also makes the compensation issue much easier to handle*).

Employees who can measure their own progress are going to develop a greater sense of **personal responsibility** and **satisfaction**.

The key to establishing effective measures for a job lies in identifying those areas an employee can **directly influence** and then ensuring **specific measurements connected to the people they are meant to help.** Failing to link measurement to relevance leads to misery.

Such measures need not be completely quantitative. Often, the most effective and appropriate measures are **behavioural in nature** and might simply call for an informal survey of customers or employees.

Summary

Dealing with the three causes of job misery will help you and your organisation build **a culture of job fulfilment** – an environment in which employees are fully engaged rather than passive doers of someone else's business.

Are you ready to start work on addressing each of the three causes? Since they are all in your control the potential for self-fulfilment is high!

READING 16

Creating Meaning at work

Roffey Park (Penna)

Meaning at Work is real. Research conducted by **Roffey Park** on behalf of Penna, the global consulting group, demonstrates that 'meaning at work' can add to the bottom line of companies. 70% of employees according to the research are looking for more 'meaning at work' the subject of the keynote speaker, Charles Handy, at last year's CIPD Conference.

But what does 'meaning at work' mean, how do you create it and what are the benefits to companies that can be bothered to provide it?

The summary of the research provides the answers and forms the content of **Reading 16**. When you consider (according to Investors in People) that 80% of staff feel motivated when they understand both where they and the organisation is going and that the figure drops to 30% when they don't it seems like 'meaning at work' is a relevant topic for management research.

The idea in brief – the 'core' idea

What constitutes 'meaning at work'. Is it just a soft, fluffy idea or is there a hard, recognisable edge to it. According to the research it has clear business benefits.

Three elements comprise 'meaning at work'. When they are aligned 'meaning at work' is likely to exist. So what are the three elements?

First, there are factors related to *the individual*:

- A sense of self (and the space to be yourself).
- A balance between work and non-work life.
- Alignment between personal and organisational values.

Secondly, there are factors related to *the organisation*:

- A sense of community (a feeling of belonging to something bigger than yourself).
- The opportunity to interact meaningfully with others.
- The opportunity to contribute to the organisation's success.
- A manager who helps to create meaning for you.

Thirdly, there are factors related to *society*:

- The opportunity to contribute outside the organisation.
- Working for an employer with a sense of corporate responsibility.

Meaning at Work exists in the area of overlap between three elements. All three sources matter and combine to create meaning.

(Nothing too difficult here. However, I suspect Picasso got huge meaning from his work but would not meet many of these criteria. But we'll leave that one for now).

The idea expanded – key findings

A sense of self (and the space to be yourself)

- 56% of senior managers and 30% of managers believe their work role is vital to their sense of identity (especially true for older employees).
- Personal success matters. 49% of respondents (74% of senior managers) found meaning in their sense of personal achievement while 45% (60% of senior managers) thrive on personal challenge.

A balance between work and non-work life

- 44% of respondents cited work-life balance as a positive experience. However, different groups find different ways of creating it (for example, senior managers – almost 50% – regard flexitime as important).

- 25% of employees were working longer hours than a year ago (even though 55% of employers recognised the importance of work-life balance).
- The opportunity to work from home, take sabbaticals, receive enhanced maternity/paternity rights were not regarded as important.

Alignment between personal and organisational values

- Values fit is becoming more important with 14% (27% for senior people) listing it as a key determinant in making a career move. However, it pales to insignificance when compared to location (49%), job content (47%) and package (44%).

A sense of community (a feeling of belonging to something bigger than yourself)

- The workplace provides a genuine sense of community for 32% of respondents (43% of employers believe they have created it).

The opportunity to interact meaningfully with others

- Social interaction with colleagues is a significant source of meaning (>50% of respondents) particularly so for women (21% v 12% for men) and the under 25s who value a network of close friends.
- 25% of respondents cite the importance of broadening their understanding and knowledge of other cultures through their job roles, especially women (30% v 17% for men) – a factor undervalued by employers in the research.

The opportunity to contribute to the organisation's success

- This is a critical source of meaning for 43% of respondents (52% for managers and 58% for more senior people).

A manager who helps to create meaning for you

- While the majority of employers believe they are providing this, 30% of the sample have not experienced it. There is room for growth.
- Women are more responsive than men to a positive management style although men (especially >55s) are more likely to appreciate integrity.

The opportunity to contribute outside the organisation

- 22% of respondents (21% of senior managers) consider the opportunity to contribute to society makes their role more meaningful. This is especially true for older workers (33%) and women (27% v 16% for men).

Working for an employer with a sense of corporate responsibility

- No quantitative data was provided by the survey for this factor

Summary

Where employees experience a sense of community, the space to be themselves and the opportunity to make a contribution they are more likely to find meaning at work according to this research conducted in 2005.

Organisations that can unlock the secret of what provides 'meaning at work' can expect *higher levels of motivation* (55% of respondents), *loyalty* (42%) and *pride in their work* (32%). It begs the usual question as to whether these lead to increased productivity and performance although there is evidence from the research that this is the case.

Younger employees (<35) are more likely to respond positively to finding 'meaning at work' than older employees and consider brand and reputation important factors. *If organisations are to attract, motivate and retain this generation they must focus more on providing 'meaning at work'.*

87% of employers recognise the importance of 'meaning at work' though may be uncertain about how to create it. They also over-estimate the extent to which it is being provided.

Aristotle probably got it right. He called it 'eudaimonia': flourishing by doing your best at what you are best at. With or without work-life balance I suspect those with 'eudaimonia' experienced 'meaning at work'.

The idea in practice – putting the idea to work

The practical implications? What one thing can I implement as a result of this research?

How applicable are these findings to you and/or your team?

1. Rank the nine factors in terms of importance to you (and/or get your team members to do the same and reach a consensus on the 'top three').
2. Take the 'top three' factors and give each a score out of 10 for the extent to which you and/or your team feel they are addressed – i.e. to what extent are you/your team experiencing 'meaning at work'?
3. If you /your team are, fine. If there are significant gaps what can you/the team do to bridge them? Be concrete and specific!

Now answer the question: What are the three most important lessons for leaders in your organisation with respect to creating 'meaning at work?'

Remember!

Creating 'meaning at work' is a high-level engagement factor that increases an organisation's attractiveness to new talent and retention of existing – the organisation becomes more engaging. The more engaged the employee, the more difficult it is for the competition to attract them. **'Creating meaning at work' is a business tool for attracting, motivating and retaining talent.**

4

Making the Team Work

Next to leadership, the second most written-about management topic is probably the fascinating but complex world of teams.

The readings that follow are summaries of a few of the gems that have appeared in recent years. All focus on how leadership teams might improve their performance, bearing in mind that we define performance as a multiple of results (WHAT has been achieved) and effectiveness (HOW the results were achieved). If there is a core message emerging from these readings it is that truly effective teams get the basics right, focus on performance in the way we define it and concentrate on teamwork rather than team building.

One of the biggest mistakes is to treat teams as generic entities. To make any progress at all on working with teams the very first question – or rather two questions – that must be addressed is 'what kind of team does the business need and what kind of team do team members want?' Only when this is clear, does it make sense to move on to how the team might work more effectively. In certain instances, the business may not actually require a team – in the full sense of the term – and members may not actually want to work in a team-based environment.

What Kind of Team?

Teams come in all shapes and sizes. For some, whole companies are the team. For others it's a tightly knit group of people engaged in a common task.

Probably the most important question is to figure out exactly what

110

kind of team is required. This is not always as easy as it sounds. At its simplest answers are needed to two important sub-questions:

Q1 What kind of team does the business need to deliver what is required?

Q2 What kind of team do the members want to motivate them to deliver what is required?

The answer to these two questions may or may not be the same. For example, the kind of team that a business needs which has a global matrix structure in place will be substantially different from a business where there are single lines of reporting and a single point of accountability. For the former, a looser working arrangement may work better, for the latter a more cohesive, tightly structured arrangement may be more suitable.

Similarly, team members will vary in their needs to be part of a fully functioning team. For some it will be central to their interpersonal needs. For others it will not feature. For some it will be in between. So while recognising that perfect design is not always possible the kind of team that is required will depend on the business situation and the needs of the people involved.

In the matrix below (Figure 6):

A *real team* is needed when both the business and the people need are high. By real team we mean a "*small* number of people with *complementary skills* who are committed to a *common purpose, performance goals* and working *approach* for which they hold themselves *mutually accountable*" (Katzenbach & Smith 1993).

111

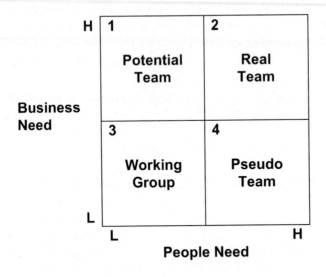

Figure 6: Four Types of Team

When the business need is high but the people need is low then we have a *potential team* – i.e. one that has the potential to become a real team. Whether this will happen will depend on the extent to which people's expectations can be realigned with those of the business. Usually, this can be achieved through a process of team development.

When the business and the people need is low a *working group* may be more appropriate. In this situation, an informal, well-functioning group of individuals work together co-operatively to provide what is needed.

When the business need is low but the people need is high then we are likely to have a *pseudo team*. It is pseudo because it is likely to engage in team-building activities in the mistaken belief that engaging in such activities is what is required to become a real team.

A real team is more likely to thrive where the business need is fully aligned with peoples' needs. Unfortunately, many businesses adopt the wrong strategies for the wrong quadrant because the value of teamwork is often regarded as more important than what the business actually requires to perform. By focusing on performance through results X effectiveness – as opposed to 'trying to become a team' – most business-critical teams can deliver outcomes that require and produce desired team behaviours. Teamwork, rather than team building, needs to be the focus of attention.

The message? Careful diagnosis up-front to ensure the right strategies for any given business-people mix. There is no team for all occasions.

Characteristics of High Performance Teams

Focusing on *performance* and *team basics* – as opposed to trying to 'become a team' – will deliver outcomes that in themselves require team behaviours. Real teams, as portrayed by Katzenbach & Smith (1993), are deeply committed to their *purpose, goals,* and *working approach.*

Teams with a shared purpose are more likely to generate *commitment* because debate is likely to be more honest and open when people feel strongly about the shared purpose. And when people are committed they are more likely to hold themselves accountable and being held *collectively accountable* is a hallmark of most high performing teams.

'Real' teams differ from 'working groups' – a working group's performance is a function of what its members do as individuals. A 'real' team's performance includes both individual *and* collective results.

In high-performance teams, members are very committed to one another's development and provide *support* when needed. Silos are simply not accepted. The team to which members belong is the 'number one' team and roles on that team are people's 'number one roles'.

The clarity and consistency of the company's overall performance standards – the 'performance ethic' – is critical to the generation of effective teams. Creating a team that delivers is always a result of pursuing a demanding *performance challenge.* Measurable, challenging performance goals apply as much to the team as to individuals. Ideally, the reward structure reflects this as well.

High performing teams agree a *working approach* – how individuals will operate together. As Katzenbach & Smith (1993) explain, this generally means members doing equal amounts of real work together. It is not about delegating and reviewing. It is about doing real work together. While sub-groups may be formed, the team as a whole is genuinely accountable for the team's performance.

Clearly, it helps if the team is the *right size*, and has the *right people on board* with the *right skills*. In teams, small is beautiful. There is a size beyond which it becomes difficult to operate as a proper team (probably >10). The team's composition should reflect the type of people needed rather than a preoccupation with being 'fair'. It is a team 'fit for purpose' that is being designed not a democracy where every part of the organisation is represented (representation can be achieved in other ways). Specialist skills can be acquired but all members should possess well-developed *interpersonal and problem-solving skills*.

Most teams can significantly enhance their performance if they are characterised by the elements described above. Focusing on performance – not chemistry, togetherness or good feelings – shapes teams more than any other factor. But performance in high performing team language is a multiplier of *both* results *and* effectiveness. Both the 'what' and the 'how' are critical if results are to be sustained beyond the short term.

The Team Performance Curve

The Team Performance Curve (see Figure 7 below), used by Katzenbach & Smith (1993), illustrates how well any small group performs will depend on the basic approach it takes and how effectively it implements that approach.

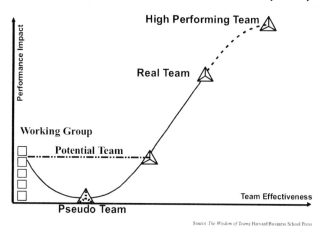

Figure 7: Team Performance Curve

(Reproduced with permission by Harvard Business School Press)

Unlike real teams, *working groups* rely primarily on the sum of individual contributions for their performance. While these may suit certain circumstances generally they will not produce the level of outstanding commitment and performance that characterises real teams. Making the transition from a working group to a real team is a challenge faced by many management teams.

Pseudo teams do all the right teamy-type things but because such activities become an end in themselves, relationships and good feelings flourish while performance often drops. A nice place to be when performance does not matter.

Potential teams avoid pseudo team status and cross the dotted line in the diagram above with a huge leap of faith. They start to climb the performance curve and inevitably take risks and confront obstacles. The danger for potential teams is that when they get stuck they slip back to pseudo team behaviour – away-day team building events, for example – rather than constantly focusing on performance. Teamwork not teambuilding is what is required for a team that is stuck.

The steepest performance gain comes between a potential team and a real team but any movement up the slope is worth pursuing. The words used by Katzenbach & Smith (1993) in their definition of a *real team* are carefully chosen: small number of people, complementary skills, committed to a common purpose, performance goals, working approach and mutually accountability.

A real team will become a truly *high performing team* when it meets all the conditions of a real team and has members who are deeply committed to one another's personal growth, development and success. The dotted line at the top part of the curve indicates the exceptional personal and team commitment required for genuine and sustainable high performance. The high performance team significantly outperforms all reasonable expectations. It is a powerful model for all real and potential teams but is only a useful weapon to deploy when the business needs it and when people really want it. Answering the question 'what kind of team' requires both honesty and a sense of realism. Too many teams have delusions of grandeur and are seduced by the language of high performance teams.

Building Team Performance

Focus on getting team basics right is the best starting point. In so doing, leaders can pay attention to the following 'top ten' tips:

- Establish urgency, demanding performance standards and direction.
- Select members for skills (potential) rather than chemistry.
- Pay special attention to first meetings and actions.
- Set clear rules of behaviour – model them – and hold members to them.
- Set and seize upon a few immediate performance tasks and goals.
- Continually challenge and stretch the group – encourage open and challenging debate.
- Spend lots of time together – especially at the beginning – to build trust.

- Exploit positive feedback, recognition and rewards where possible.
- Expect set-backs – be prepared to return to basics.
- Remembering to celebrate success.

The role of the leader is critical especially in the early stages. Good team leaders do not get in the way. They are also good players – that is to say they have credibility because team members recognise their credentials in whatever their core expertise is. You are more likely to lead an effective sales team if people recognise you have been an exceptional salesperson. Team leaders must strive to achieve a balance between *vision* (i.e. providing direction), building and sustaining *commitment* (i.e. getting people aligned behind the vision) and ensuring *execution* (i.e. providing the necessary management discipline to make sure things get done. Throughout, they must demonstrate their character by role modelling those *personal and professional qualities* that differentiate them from those who are not in leadership positions.

READING 17

Teams at the Top

McKinsey Research

In a piece of focused research in the consumer goods industry, McKinsey demonstrated that results (i.e. total returns to shareholders) were always worse *after* the arrival of a new CEO.

They use the analysis to explode the myth of heroic leadership stating that "in reality, long term success depends on the whole leadership team, for it has a broader and deeper reach into the organisation than the CEO does and its performance has a multiplier effect".

To be sure, a single person can make a difference at times but even heroic veterans such as Jack Welch emphasise the power of team leadership in action.

Reading 17 focuses on 'teamwork at the top' summarising the insights and practical implications related to a study involving 500 executives in diverse private-and-public sector organisations.

The idea in brief – the 'core' idea

Often, the leadership team is at best a collection of strong individuals who sometimes work at cross-purposes rather than a top team. When top teams gel they tend to address business performance issues directly but behavioural disorders indirectly. In other words, effectiveness is not improved by behavioural change programmes but by team members working collectively on business critical issues that *require* productive behaviours for the issues themselves to be addressed.

To meet this goal, teams – according to the research – must master three dimensions of effectiveness:

D1   A common direction – a shared understanding of goals and values.

D2   Skills of interaction – to solve complex problems and for people to take their cues from the top.

D3   The ability to renew – to expand capabilities in response to change.

Direction, interaction and renewal are interdependent and teams need to proceed simultaneously on all three fronts to make real progress.

The idea expanded – key findings

D1 A Common Direction

Many business leaders assume that they and their top teams share a common understanding of goals and values but several realities tend to undermine this:

• **Lack of alignment.** Executives may nod their heads when strategic priorities are discussed but often the team lacks a shared view of how to implement them (even if they really agree in the first place).

• **Lack of understanding.** Or more precisely, depth of understanding when the team agrees the plans but takes actions that are inconsistent because the assumptions and rationale behind the plan are not fully explored.

• **Lack of strategic focus.** Teams without a common direction simply spend more time on 'business as usual' or 'fire-fighting' than on 'doing work only they can do'.

D2 Ineffective Interaction

Many teams espouse the importance of interaction but theories in use indicate the opposite with working styles that inhibit candid communications and collaboration:

- **Poor dialogue.** When individual team members don't know each other or there is a history of conflict, games get played and mistrust creeps in. For 65% of respondents in the research data basic trust was a real issue.

- **Dysfunctional behaviour.** Poor dialogue leads to an inability to capitalise on diverse viewpoints and backgrounds thus reducing the team's ability to work creatively and adapt to changes in the market. Many executives have climbed functional silos and are accustomed to defending their organisational (*and sometimes psychological: Ed*) turf making the leap to broad strategic issues much more difficult.

D3 Inability to Renew

- **Personal dissatisfaction.** 25% of respondents said that their work did not stretch them. Collectively and individually, team members ignore new sources of ideas and information that could push them out of their comfort zones. Complacency sets in and ingrained habits fester.

- **Insularity.** Lacking information and fresh inputs from outside means most teams don't find the time to generate a real strategic focus. Internal matters divert energy from decision-making rooted in external reality.

- **Deficient skills.** Unlike middle managers who frequently get broad training and coaching senior managers often work without such a safety net. 80% of interviewees believed they had the necessary skills but only 30% believed the same of their colleagues.

The idea in practice – putting the idea to work

The practical implications? What one thing can I implement as a result of this research?

So how do you become an effective top team?

According to the researchers four strategies that replicate the way senior executives actually work together stand the best chance of building team performance (rather than 'behavioural improvement programmes'):

1. **Address a number of initiatives concurrently**

   The top team must focus on work that only it can do together. This includes framing strategy, managing performance, managing stakeholders and reviewing top talent.

2. **Channel the team's discontent**

   Only 20% of those surveyed thought their team was a high-performing one. Successful teams invite external challenges, focus on competitive threats and judge themselves by best external practice that raises the quality and sharpness of debate by 'putting the facts on the table'.

3. **Minimise outside intrusions**

   Some form of facilitation is usually required but often it works best if the outside coach or facilitator observes the team doing real work rather than directly facilitating it. Teams must discover what works for them.

4. **Encourage inquiry and reflection**

   Over 80% of respondents said insufficient time was set aside to analyse root causes. Drawing lessons from collective experience in a purposeful and structured way can have an effect in three months. Developing rules of thumb slowly and subconsciously is not an option with the tenure of CEOs becoming shorter and investors' expectations continually rising.

What does it look like in practice?

CEOs and senior executives address a number of strands of business but focus on key strategic issues by *working together as colleagues* rather than delegating to staff, consultants or individual team members.

At a minimum, say the researchers the team should spend one day each month together *doing real work as a team* perhaps being observed by a professional coach. Sub-groups of two-three members should be working together a couple of times a week on the issues identified by the team.

Teamwork is a pragmatic enterprise that grows from tangible achievements. By doing real work on important problems and applying business judgement to reflect on that work, top teams can *jump-start their performance* and *satisfy their need for visible progress.*

By using the process of observation and reflection the team can address their behaviour with less risk of personal or destructive confrontation because it takes place more objectively *after the event.*

The prize for building effective top teams is clear: they develop better strategies, perform more consistently and increase the confidence of stakeholders. They get positive results and make work satisfying both for the team members and the people they lead.

So how well is your top team doing?

READING 18

Senior leadership teams – what it takes to make them great

Ruth Wageman, Debra A. Nunes, James A. Burruss & J. Richard Hackman

What does it take to make a leadership team great?

In a study of 120 senior leadership teams from around the world covering a range of industries, countries and organisations, four Harvard researchers attempt to answer the question.

They do so comprehensively and rigorously.

Reading 18 summarises the key facets of the research outlined in their recent book *Senior Leadership Teams: What it takes to make them great*, Harvard Business School Press 2008 (permission gained for this adapted excerpt).

The idea in brief – the 'core' idea

The authors first pose a critical question: **Do you need and want a leadership team** (see below: The idea in practice – putting the idea to work)?

By leadership team they mean a **team that makes the small number of critical decisions that are most consequential for the enterprise as a whole.**

This is in contrast to other types of teams: informational teams, consultative teams or co-ordinating teams for example. A 'real' team is therefore one that makes **enterprise-related decisions**.

Using surveys, interviews and direct observation to study what differentiated superb leadership from struggling ones the researchers identified **six conditions** that CEOs could put in place to increase their chances of creating an outstanding team.

Three are essentials and three are enablers:

Essentials

- Creating a real team with clear and stable membership
- Articulating a clear and compelling direction
- Getting the right people on the team

Enablers

- Giving the team with a good structure
- Providing support resources
- Coaching the team as a team

The same process can be used to relaunch a team that is struggling, facing changed market conditions or trying to achieve a new purpose.

The idea expanded – key findings

Essentials 1: Creating a real team with clear and stable membership

What makes a group of executives a real team?

The research shows that what makes the difference between a loose agglomeration and a real team is a leader who treats the team as an entity and puts in place three essential characteristics:

- **Interdependency** – In real teams, members share responsibility for achieving a collective purpose. They are still responsible for their individual roles but they also work together, rely on one another and use each other's experience, energy, and expertise to accomplish a collective, enterprise-affecting purpose.

- **Bounded** – Real leadership teams have clear boundaries. Team members as well as outside observers know who is on the team and who isn't.

- **Stable** – Real teams maintain a stable membership long enough to get to know one another's special strengths and limitations and to learn how to work together well as a team.

Essentials 2: Articulating a clear and compelling direction

To get it right, CEOs must articulate to their teams a purpose that is **consequential, challenging and clear**. They need to be brought to life in unique ways for every leadership team.

Of the three qualities of a great leadership team, establishing clarity is the hardest. To get to clarity:

- Identify the **interdependencies** among team members that move the strategy forward. What is it that requires all the leaders to be at the table?

- Create a short list of **decisions** and actions that the team must achieve. What are the **mission-critical things** that can be done *only* by this team?

- Raise the list to a **thematic and compelling** level so that it guides team decisions and actions.

- Use **leader authority** to articulate the purpose to the team. Only the leader can establish the purpose. Others can help to refine it but ultimately it's the leader's responsibility.

Essentials 3: Getting the right people on the team

Put simply, the task is to ensure that the best players are on board. If the team is to be effective members must collectively understand and be able to represent the entire organisation (this does not mean every Tom, Dick and Harry has a seat at the table to avoid hurt feelings). **The first priority in choosing core members should be the expertise they bring to the party.**

Members of senior teams must also conceive of their role as leading in ways **that maximise the effectiveness of the organisation as a whole**. In other words, to possess a self-image as an executive leader.

Senior leadership teams also benefit from a **high level of conceptual thinking** by their members. This involves the ability to synthesise complex information from divergent sources and distil the implications for the business.

Finally, members of senior teams that make enterprise-wide decisions must be able to **engage in robust discussions**. Indeed, the ability to have such discussions is a sure sign of leadership team effectiveness. **Empathy** and **integrity** are required to ensure that conflictual situations can be handled without resorting to soft diplomacy.

Together, these three 'essentials' comprise the engine for effective team functioning. To ensure that the engine runs smoothly requires a high-grade fuel. Three 'enablers' provide the quality of fuel needed.

Enabler 1: Giving the team a good structure

The research showed that the quality of the team's structure more than any other of the six conditions determines which teams are outstanding and which are not. Three elements are critical:

- Performing **genuinely meaningful team tasks** – i.e. a concrete piece of work that the team performs together.

- The presence of **clear norms of conduct** – shared expectations about member behaviour – had the largest impact of any sub-feature of the six conditions on whether a leadership team was effective.

- For teams that must make collective decisions small is beautiful. **Keep the team size small.**

Enabler 2: Providing support resources

Four types of support were identified in the research:

- Rewards. Implementing reward strategies that recognise and reinforce team members for delivering on the team's accountabilities.

- **Information.** Data tailored to the team's needs – including measures that allow members to assess their performance *as a team*.

- **Education.** Developing the team's capabilities notwithstanding the seniority. This may be technical or behavioural.

- **Resources.** The best CEOs make sure that the team has the basic materials needed for collaborative work including time, space, staff support as well as the more mundane material resources.

Enabler 3: Coaching the team as a team

By team coaching the researchers **mean directly intervening in the process that the team uses to interact** rather than team bonding type activities.

A good coach will hold up a mirror to the team to reflect back the collective behaviours that advance and hinder teamwork. The best coaching will take place behind the closed doors of the meeting room itself not on a weekend retreat or team-away day separated from the real work of the team.

Timing is critical. Beginnings, calendar midpoints and project/task cycle ends provide special opportunities for team coaching – motivational (beginnings), consultative (midpoints) and educational (ends) inputs are especially helpful at each of these times. Do not skimp on coaching.

The idea in practice – putting the idea to work

The practical implications? What one thing can I implement as a result of this research?

Does the organisation that you lead or are part of actually need a leadership team?

Part 1: Which of the following apply?

- Significant growth/retraction.
- Horizontal integration of semiautonomous units.
- Major changes in capital or other resources.
- Externally originated challenges to traditional ways of operating.

If none apply you probably do not need a leadership team.

Part 2: What leadership functions need to be fulfilled collaboratively?

- Information exchange among senior leaders that is essential for alignment.
- Consultation for strategic and complex decisions.
- Co-ordination of a key change initiative or interdependent operations.
- Decision making about critical enterprise issues.
- If two or fewer of the above apply you probably do not need a leadership team.

If you do need a leadership team, how do you currently rate against the three 'essentials' and three 'enablers' described above? **How will you make your leadership team great?**

READING 19

Improving the performance of top teams

Andrew J. Ward et al

Differences in organisational values within a top management team can impair how the group functions, with *perceived* differences having much larger repercussions than real ones if the results of a research survey involving CEOs of 31 U.S. companies and 133 members of top management teams are to be believed. This **Reading** summarises the key findings and offers practical suggestions for addressing the issues raised in this recent research.

(See *MIT Sloan Review,* Spring 2007, for full details of the research. Also published in the Journal of Managerial Issues).

The idea in brief – the 'core' idea

Although executives on top management teams may strive to achieve common goals for their organisations in reality they represent powerful sub-units (even warring factions) with distinct group identities that can trigger conflicts and self-interested behaviours.

To examine whether differences in organisational values exist in top teams the research investigated the importance of 16 organisational values (for example, customer service, profit maximisation, reputation etc) to CEOs and members of their top teams.

The values were presented to the CEOs who were asked to indicate their level of agreement using a 1 (strongly disagree) to 7 (strongly agree) scale.

The same 16 values were presented to the top management team members who were asked for two sets of ratings: the first to indicate their own level of agreement with the values and the second to indicate their perceptions of how important the values were to their CEO. As a result, two types of dissimilarity were calculated: the *perceived value dissimilarity* and the *actual value dissimilarity*.

Study participants were also asked about their team environment, specifically *task and relationship conflict*, about *leadership effectiveness, satisfaction with the team* and *organisational commitment.*

The key findings that follow demonstrate the importance of managing perceptions in the team if dysfunctional relationship conflicts are to be avoided

The idea expanded – key findings

Perceived difference in organisational values

The members of the top teams perceived **considerable differences between their own values and that of their CEOs.** Specifically, team members rated **profit maximisation, innovation** and **customer service** as their 'top three' values.

But they *perceived* that their CEOs would favour **organisational growth, value to the community and industry leadership.**

Perception versus reality

In fact, those perceptions did not match reality. CEOs actual ratings indicated **reputation of the firm, integrity** and **innovation** as their real 'top three'. Indeed, for about half of the 16 values members of the team *overestimated* the differences (in terms of importance) between their own values and those of their CEOs and for about half they *underestimated* (in terms of importance) the differences. People's perceptions were clearly off.

The impact of value differences

The study looked at two types of conflict: *task* (characterised by substantive, issue-related differences in opinion) and *relationship* (characterised by disagreements over personalised, individually oriented matters).

When organisational values are perceived to be at odds with a person's own beliefs, the incongruity can lead to both task as well as relationship conflict. If the conflict is allowed to escalate the result can be destructive and costly (think recent events at The Walt Disney Company).

The study results show that perception rather than reality drive behaviour. Specifically, the greater the *perceived* difference in values between members of a top team and their CEO the greater the conflict. *Actual* differences were not a significant factor.

In other words, perception becomes reality in terms of driving executive behaviour. Beliefs rule OK.

The importance of leadership

Not surprisingly, both task and relationship conflict can affect the satisfaction and commitment of team members with *relationship conflict* being the more destructive when there are perceived value differences. This was especially true in teams where the CEO was also rated low on *leadership effectiveness*. The importance of creating 'followship' should not be underestimated.

Perceived differences in organisation values also had a direct effect on members' *commitment*. When there is misalignment, team members become disengaged. When consensus and commitment are seen to be lacking in the executive team, work climate, co-operation and employee trust throughout the organisation deteriorate.

Summary

It is imperative that companies manage the alignment of values among top management team members in ways that reduce dysfunctional relationship conflicts within the team while promoting those task-related conflicts that ultimately lead to smarter ideas and better business decisions.

* Adapted excerpts from Improving the Performance of Top Teams by Andrew L Ward, Melenie J Lankau, Allen C Amason, Jeffrey A Sonnenfeld and Bradley R Agle. MIT Sloan Management Review (Spring 2007) by permission of publisher. © 2007 by Massachusetts Institute of Technology. All rights reserved.

The idea in practice – putting the idea to work

The practical implications? What one thing can I implement as a result of this research?

While differences in organisational values among top team members and their leader are unavoidable such differences should not necessarily lead to conflicts that are unproductive and damaging. To prevent such conflicts it is important to:

- **Establish the right climate** in the team so that misperceptions are kept to a minimum (for example, increase people's familiarity with each other so they feel easier about voicing dissenting views. Offsites and work projects that require people to interact collectively can go a long way toward establishing the right atmosphere). The primary responsibility for creating an environment that encourages candid discussion lies with the CEO or team leader.

- **Make the decision-making process transparent and fair** so that people can still feel the value of their input to the decision even when their ideas are not fully adopted. Agreeing collectively the criteria to be used is one way of ensuring this. Relationship conflict will hamper effective decision-making.

- **Understand and manage perceptions** to ensure everyone is on the same page. The CEO or team leader must clearly articulate what's important to them and correct any misperceptions people may have. Only then can true differences be addressed. The CEO should never assume they have been clear about their organisational values or that everyone perceives them in the same way.

READING 20

Engaging leadership in high performance teams

Professor Alimo-Metcalfe & Margaret Bradley

The piece of research summarised in **Reading 20** presents hard evidence that employee engagement may actually work.

The research carried out by Professor Alimo-Metcalfe and Margaret Bradley in 46 NHS front-line teams over a three period demonstrated not only that work attitudes improve but productivity and performance as well (go to www.sdo.Ishtm.ac.uk/sdo222002.html. for more).*

Note: OED Consulting is familiar with Alimo-Metcalfe's previous research – for example, her work on the development of a UK-based Transformational Leadership Questionnaire (TLQ). The research is rigorous and strongly linked to practical outcomes for those in leadership roles.

The idea in brief – the 'core' idea

Three dimensions of leadership were identified as a result of the research:

- **Leadership capabilities** – the degree to which members saw their team as competent in leadership.
- **Visionary leadership** – the degree to which the team is seen as displaying 'visionary leadership'.
- **Engaging with others** – the degree to which the team demonstrated engaging leadership behaviours.

All three dimensions positively and significantly impacted on employees attitudes to work but **only 'engaging with others' significantly affected all aspects of attitudes to work and well-being at work, including a strong sense of team spirit**.

Furthermore, unlike the other two dimensions, 'engaging with others' was identified as **a significant predictor of performance** thus establishing an evidence-based link between leadership behaviour and organisational performance.

The idea expanded – key findings

The teams that had succeeded in developing an engaging leadership style displayed the following characteristics:

- Engaging stakeholders at the outset to shape the nature of the service to be provided.
- Ensuring that a collective vision of good quality service was shaped and owned by team members.
- Encouraging team members to take the lead where and when it was appropriate for them to do so.
- Creating a culture of joint problem-solving that empowered team members to take the risks necessary to be innovative.
- Consulting team members on impending changes and taking their responses into consideration.

So what does an 'engaging' leadership style actually mean in practice?

The researchers list the following items:

- Showing concerns for the needs of staff.
- Empowering people by trusting them to make decisions.
- Listening to others' ideas and being willing to accommodate them.
- Finding time to discuss problems and issues.
- Supporting others by coaching and mentoring.
- Inspiring staff to contribute fully to the work of the team.
- Actively promoting the achievements of the team externally.

What this research demonstrates is that when competent, visionary leaders successfully *engage with others* the overall

impact on attitudes to work, well-being at work and team performance is highly likely to be positive.

* Reading published with the permission of Professor Alimo-Metcalfe

The idea in practice – putting the idea to work

The practical implications? What one thing can I implement as a result of this research?

Clearly, engaging with others' focuses on what might be regarded as the 'softer' side of leadership reminiscent of Robert Greenleaf's concept of 'servant leadership' which is not to everyone's taste (*probably of greater appeal to those engaged in public services: Ed*).

However, there are many business situations (e.g. investment banks) where – at least based on this author's experience – applying such practices would help address some of the frustration felt by competent junior staff as well as the retention levels experienced by the teams in which they work.

Moreover, transferring good practice from the public to the private sector may actually help improve private sector performance if the results of this research are anything to go by.

There is one caveat, however, that the researchers make; **for the effects of engagement to be sustained it is critical to embed the behaviours required in the culture of the organisation.** Which takes us back, as it usually does, to the CEO and the top team and the extent to which they are willing and able to take on board findings such as these.

If they do, then the effects, according to the researchers' experience can be extraordinary.

In the meantime, why not start experimenting with the people in your team?

READING 21

The five dysfunctions of a team

Patrick Lencioni

Next to leadership, the second most written-about management topic is probably the fascinating but complex world of teams.

Among the plethora of books, articles and research occasionally, just occasionally, a gem, a useful nugget appears.

One such book, which has driven a lot of OED's thinking on teams, is The Wisdom of Teams based on research carried out by two McKinsey consultants back in the 1990s. However, the focus of this **Reading** is a more recent work: *The Five Dysfunctions of a Team* written in compelling, story-telling form by Patrick Lencioni, author of best-selling 'The Five Temptations of a CEO' and published by Jossey-Bass *

For new leaders – or indeed experienced leaders who feel things are not quite as they should be in their team – Lencioni distils the issues that keep teams from realising their full potential offering practical 'how-to' solutions that help move teams up the performance curve by significantly improving their effectiveness.

The idea in brief – the 'core' idea

Organisations fail to achieve teamwork because they (unknowingly) fall prey to five natural but dangerous pitfalls: *the five dysfunctions of a team.* They are not separate, independent issues but rather an interrelated model making susceptibility to even one of them potentially lethal for the success of the team.

So what are these 'pitfalls'?

1. The first dysfunction is an **absence of trust** among team members. Essentially, the author says, this stems from their unwillingness to be vulnerable. Team members who are not

136

genuinely open with one another about their mistakes and weaknesses make it impossible to build a foundation of trust.

(Trust is the confidence among team members that their colleagues' intentions are good and that there is no reason to be protective or careful around the group – i.e. team members must be comfortable being vulnerable with one another in order to act without concern for self-protection. Then they can focus energies on the job at hand rather than on being strategically disingenuous or political with one another).

2. This failure to build trust is damaging because it sets the tone for the second dysfunction: **fear of conflict**. Teams that lack trust are incapable of engaging in unfiltered and passionate debates of ideas. Instead, they resort to veiled discussions and guarded comments. They cannot discuss the undiscussable.

(Contrary to the notion that teams waste time and energy arguing, those that smooth over or avoid the real issues doom themselves to revisiting issues again and again without successful resolution).

3. A lack of healthy conflict is an issue because it ensures the third dysfunction of a team: **lack of commitment**. Without having aired their opinions through passionate debate team members rarely, if ever, buy in and commit to decisions even though they may espouse agreement during meetings.

(Great teams make clear and timely decisions and move forward with complete buy-in including those who were against the decision. Seeking consensus is one of the key causes of lack of commitment because business reality dictates that complete agreement is rarely possible. What matters is that everyone feels their views have been heard, understood and taken into account).

4. When there is lack of commitment and buy-in team members develop an **avoidance of accountability**, the fourth dysfunction. Without committing to a clear course of action even the most focused and driven people hesitate to challenge their colleagues

on issues and behaviours that seem counterproductive to the good of the team.

(In the context of teamwork accountability refers to the willingness and courage of team members to challenge their peers on performance or behaviours that might damage the effectiveness of the team. It also means that team members are collectively responsible for the output and performance of the team.)

5. This failure to hold one another accountable creates an environment where the fifth dysfunction can thrive. **Inattention to results** occurs when team members put their individual needs (ego, careers, etc.) or the needs of their own team/unit above the goals of the team. In short, they do not regard the team of which they are a member as their 'first team'.

(The ultimate dysfunction of a team is the tendency of members to care about something other than the collective goals of the group. An unrelenting focus on specific objectives and clearly defined outcomes is a requirement for any team that judges itself on performance. No amount of trust, conflict, commitment or accountability can compensate for the lack of desire to win that sets great teams apart).

The idea expanded – key findings

For each of the five dysfunctions there are several strategies and tactics outlined in the book for overcoming them. But paramount is *the role of the leader*. What part can s/he play to ensure that any one of the five dysfunctions described above does not derail the team?

Absence of Trust

The most important action that a leader can take is to demonstrate vulnerability first. This requires that the leader risks losing face in front of the team so that team members will take the same risks themselves. Such displays of vulnerability (witnessed many times by this MRU author) cannot be 'staged' – in fact, the surest way to lose trust is to feign vulnerability in order to manipulate the emotions of others. It simply doesn't work.

(By building trust the leader makes conflict possible because team members do not hesitate to engage in robust and open debate).

Fear of Conflict

One of the most natural responses of a leader is to try and protect members from harmful conflict by trying to intervene too readily. This prevents members from developing their own conflict-management skills and stifles the very things that need to be brought out into the open. Therefore it is vital that leaders show restraint when their people engage in conflict and allow resolution to occur as naturally as possible. A leader's ability to model appropriate conflict behaviour is essential – by avoiding or clumsily intervening a team leader will simply encourage this dysfunction to thrive.

(By engaging in productive conflict a team can more readily buy into a decision knowing that they have heard and benefited from everyone's ideas).

Lack of Commitment

More than any other member of the team the leader must be comfortable with the prospect of making a decision that is wrong. Effective teams unite behind decisions even when there is little assurance about the correctness of the decision. They do this because they know that in the business world a decision is often better than *no* decision. They realise that it is better to make a clear-cut decision and be wrong – and then change direction with equal boldness – than it is to fudge, waffle and compromise.

(So that team members challenge each other on their behaviours and actions they need a sense of what is expected. You cannot seriously hold someone accountable for something that was never bought in to or made clear in the first place).

Avoidance of Accountability

To instil accountability on a team the leader has to encourage and allow the team to serve as the first and primary accountability mechanism. Once such a climate of accountability has been established the leader must be willing to act as the ultimate arbiter of discipline when the team itself fails (which should be a rare occurrence). Accountability in this sense is not relegated to a consensus approach but rather to a shared team responsibility within which the leader will not hesitate to step in if it becomes necessary.

(If team members are not being held accountable for team contributions they will turn their attention to their own needs. Individual agendas then take over from the focus on collective results).

Inattention to Results

More than any of the other dysfunctions the leader sets the tone for performance and results almost to the extent that 'performance drives teamwork' rather than 'teamwork drives performance'. If there is any hint, any suggestion, that the leader values anything other than performance they will take that as permission to do the same for themselves. Huge recognition – both financial and non-financial – should be given to members who contribute most significantly to group results.

Teamwork ultimately boils down to practising a small set of consistent principles – call them 'team basics' if you will – over a prolonged period of time. This is more a question of embracing common sense with uncommon discipline and persistence than applying complex theories.

But in the end, teams succeed because they are human. By recognising human imperfections members of functional teams overcome the natural tendencies that make trust, conflict, commitment, accountability and a focus on results so elusive.

* *The Five Dysfunctions of a Team*, Patrick Lencioni. © Patrick Lencioni, 2002. Reproduced with permission of John Wiley & Sons Inc.

The idea in practice – putting the idea to work

The practical implications? What one thing can I implement as a result of this research?

Get hold of the book and complete the 15-statement questionnaire provided by the author to make an assessment of your own team (perhaps having each team member complete it). When you have done this, share the results with the team focusing on the following questions:

Q1 Based on these (albeit crude) results what kind of team have we got? How do we want it to be different?

Q2 What specific actions should the team take to overcome the lowest scoring dysfunction(s)?

Q3 What specific actions should the leader take to overcome the lowest scoring dysfunction(s)?

Q4 What other actions should the team and/or the leader take to ensure that functionality is sustained over time?

READING 22

Making virtual teams work

John Symons & Claudia Stenzel

The focus of this **Reading** is **virtual teams,** distilling theory with recent research findings published by John Symons and Claudia Stenzel in the Spring issue of the *Journal of General Management* (Vol. 32 No. 3). *

What do we mean by a *virtual team*? The term is used to describe **project teams working across time and space using electronic media.**

Virtual teams are characterised by geographically dispersed members working on a specific project using computer-supported software to facilitate interaction between team members.

The often 'ad hoc' team members are likely to represent different specialist functions and to have multiple reporting lines. Unified by the project they typically use telephone and videoconferences as well as email and other more sophisticated groupware technologies to communicate.

Making virtual teams work is potentially difficult because it requires *collaboration, co-operation, co-ordination and commitment* from team members who are working physically apart. Not surprisingly, **understanding how to lead a virtual team is becoming a fundamental competence for managers in global organisations.**

Virtual teaming has attractive potential benefits. In particular, improved resource utilisation through greater flexibility and human resource availability regardless of location. However, **dysfunctional cross-cultural conflicts amplify the risks of failure for multinational virtual teams.**

Understanding why people may or may not work successfully together in a virtual team enables team performance to be improved.

The idea in brief – the 'core' idea

The key competencies necessary for effective virtual team working identified by the authors can be clustered under three headings: *technology, leadership and culture.*

The research emphasises the singular importance of leadership and culture:

"As long as the technology works and the users know what, when and how to use it effectively, the issues of fundamental importance lie in human resource management."

What it takes to make virtual teams succeed is 10% technology and 90% people.

The idea expanded – key findings

Leadership and communication

- Without the face-to-face social exchanges and visual clues of traditional leadership, the emergent leader has to rely more on *influence and facilitation skills.*

- *The start of the project is critical.* Virtual team leaders need to be able to:
  - select team members for the task
  - employ the right computer-mediated technology
  - get a team started
  - define the team's purpose and operating methods
  - gain commitment
  - determine measures of success
  - establish effective communication practices between team members

- Human communication is an important aspect of virtual teaming. It is a virtual leader's challenge to *build and maintain a trust-based culture.*

Trust in virtual teams

Face-to-face relationships have no equal and virtual teams are most vulnerable to dysfunctional conflict when team members are unfamiliar with one another. **Trust is the foundation for performance in a virtual team environment.**

Three building blocks are required to create trust:

- *Confidence* in the skills and potential performance of the team and its members.
- *Integrity*, which means trust on the basis of credibility and honesty.
- *Relationship*, which means the concern for the wellbeing of others.

Initial impressions are formed quickly and last. **It is therefore critical that virtual team leaders make personal meetings possible at least at the start of the team's existence.** Commitment and effort are required.

Culture

The structure of virtual teams is usually less strong than that of co-located teams because individual performance cannot be monitored closely due to the physical dispersion of team members. *The concept of the working day is rapidly becoming meaningless.*

While valuing diversity is essential inevitably team members will have to deviate from their own culturally determined behaviours and adapt new ones.

Members of virtual teams need to share the feeling of 'globalness'. **Virtual culture needs to be 'in sync' with the corporate culture and strategy of the organisation** that may be difficult in organisations characterised by several cultures.

Conflict in virtual teams

Where groups or individuals have different values and assumptions then these may well compete and create conflict. **In multinational virtual teams this tends to be exacerbated by the inability to** observe and interpret clues from other cultures. But when such conflict is well managed, culturally diverse teams are more likely to engage in innovative 'out-of-the box' thinking.

Ensuring that team members are 'cross-culturally trained' will greatly assist the smooth working of a virtual team as will an acceptance that those working in virtual teams will have to adopt new behaviours that fit better with the needs of the virtual world they have joined. **Flexibility, sensitivity and a willingness to experiment and learn are required attributes of potential virtual team members.**

The simple technique of keeping logs (electronic) journals to record actions and reflections will greatly assist learning and improvement. **Tracking what works and what doesn't helps to create problem-awareness and helps team leaders to prevent cross-cultural conflict from occurring, or at least minimises its presence.**

* Published with permission from Braybrooke Press.

The idea in practice – putting the idea to work

The practical implications? What one thing can I implement as a result of this research?

- Recognise that technology is merely an enabler; successful **virtual teams are about people.**
- Effective virtual teams need **good communication** rather than IT skills.
- The team leader must **define the team's purpose and operating procedures** (including communication practices).
- Where possible use **face-to-face** meetings for resolving conflict
- Use **shared** rather than imposed leadership.
- Conduct a **cultural 'due diligence'** at the start of the project to help members recognise and value differences.
- Establish **trust** across the team.
- **Avoid viewing team members through national cultural stereotypes** by understanding the individuals and their values in the virtual team.

- **Value diversity.**
- Learn some **cultural frameworks/models** (e.g. Hofstede, Trompenaars).

Conclusion

Through electronic media we are becoming virtually borderless. But this will not happen effectively without a concern for working practices in the virtual team. Virtual teaming is different from face-to-face working. It relies heavily on trust and the recognition of cultural differences that can be harnessed to improve the team's output especially in the forming stage of a new team. But it takes time to prepare the foundations for cross-cultural understanding – time that will be rewarded in the later stages. The better we do this, the more the gap will be narrowed between face-to-face and virtual working.

READING 23

Big teams

Lynda Gratton & Tamara Erickson

In another life the author was a member of a *very* large project team working for a very large and *very* well known public corporation. The problem was it never *felt* like a *team* so never really performed like a great team should.

Recent research conducted across 55 large teams in 15 multinational companies by Lynda Gratton and Tamara Erickson at the London Business School provides many of the answers the author was searching for at the time. (For a full outline of the research, see *Harvard Business Review*, November 2007 – permission gained from HBSP for this adapted excerpt).

Using statistical analyses the researchers considered more than 100 factors that might contribute to successful collaboration across large, often virtual teams. From these, eight practices were identified that correlated with success – that is, helped teams overcome the difficulties that were posed by size, long-distance communication, diversity and specialisation.

The eight practices fall into four categories that form the core of **Reading 23**.

The idea in brief – the 'core' idea

The core idea is essentially a *paradox*. Major, global-scale initiatives require large teams.

But teams that are large, virtual, diverse and composed of highly talented specialists with expectations to match are the very teams that make it hard to get anything done. In other words, **the very qualities required for success are the same qualities that undermine success.**

For example. As the size of the team expands – sometimes to 100 or more – the tendency to collaborate naturally decreases. Similarly, as teams become more virtual, co-operation declines. As for diversity, while the very nature of the task requires it research shows that it is people who are alike that collaborate more easily. With respect to expertise, the greater proportion of experts in a team the more likely it is to disintegrate or reach a stalemate.

The key issue for executives is how to strengthen an organisation's ability to perform complex collaborative tasks – to maximise the effectiveness of large, diverse teams – while minimising the disadvantages posed by their structure and composition.

The key findings below are intended to throw light on this important question.

The idea expanded – key findings

Category 1: Executive Support

At the most basic level, a team's success or failure at collaborating reflects the philosophy of the top executives. Where executives invest in supporting relationships and demonstrate collaborative behaviours themselves then teams are more likely to do well.

Three practices comprise executive support:

- **Investing in signature relationship practices**

  Executives can encourage collaborative behaviours by **making highly visible investments** that demonstrate their commitment to collaboration. This might be something as simple as facilities with open floor plans and layouts that foster communications between key groups or individuals. For example, when one firm of management consultants took over another firm the employees of the latter were spread across the merged organisation to foster integration and share professional practices.

- **Modelling collaborative behaviours**

  At companies where the senior executives demonstrate highly collaborative behaviours themselves, teams collaborate well.

For example, at a north American bank where historically there had been conflict between two departments – partly due to differing objectives and partly due to personalities – the new head of one of the departments took it upon himself to visibly collaborate with the other department so that members of his team would do the same. As a result, the number of commercial deals won rose considerably.

- **Creating a 'gift culture'**

  Mentoring and coaching – especially on an informal basis – help people to build the networks they need to work across corporate boundaries. For example, at Nokia, informal mentoring is part of the culture. As soon as someone joins the recruiting manager helps the employee establish a professional and social network – names, topics for discussion and why the relationship might be important.

Category 2: Focused HR Practices

Contrary to expectations most formal HR programmes (for example, the type of reward system) had little effect on collaboration. The two practices that did were training in skills related to collaboration and support for informal community building.

- **Ensuring the requisite skills**

  HR departments that teach employees how to build relationships, communicate well and resolve conflicts creatively can have a major impact on team collaboration.
  PWC and Lehmann Brothers are cited as benchmark organisations in terms of having some of the strongest capabilities in collaboration reflected in the range and quality of their skills training.

- **Supporting a strong sense of community**

  When people feel a strong sense of community they are more comfortable reaching out to others and more likely to share knowledge. For example, teams at ABM Amro rated the company's support for informal communities very positively making the technology needed for long distance collaboration readily available to groups with shared interests.

Category 3: The Right Leaders

In groups with high collaborative behaviours the team leaders clearly made a difference. The most distinguishing feature of such leaders lay in their flexibility.

- **Assigning team leaders that are both task-and relationship-oriented**

  The debate has traditionally been focused on whether a task or a relationship orientation creates a better leader but in fact both re key to success. **Typically, leaning more heavily on a task orientation at the outset of a project and shifting toward a relationship orientation once the work is in full swing works best.** At Marriott, evidence of both kinds of capabilities becomes a significant criterion on which people are selected for key leadership roles.

Category 4: Team Formation and Structure

The final set of lessons for developing and managing complex teams has to do with the makeup and structure of the teams themselves.

- **Building on heritage relationships**

  When too many team members are strangers, people may be reluctant to share knowledge. The best practice is to put at least a few people who know one another on the team. Nokia, for example, has developed architecture designed to make good use of heritage relationships. When it needs to transfer skills across business functions or units it moves entire small teams intact instead of reshuffling individuals into new positions.

- **Understanding role clarity and task ambiguity**

  Co-operation increases when the roles of individual team

members are sharply defined yet the team is given latitude on how to achieve the task. For example, at Reuters successful teams worked out of far-flung locations often not speaking a common language. Individuals were given autonomy for discrete pieces of a project thus being encouraged to work independently within the overall team goal.

The idea in practice – putting the idea to work

The practical implications? What one thing can I implement as a result of this research?

Before starting to assemble and manage a team ask: *how complex is the collaborative task?*

If more than two of the following statements are true the task probably requires complex collaboration and attention should therefore be given to the factors outlined above:

- The task is unlikely to be accomplished successfully using only the skills within the team.
- The task must be addressed by a new group formed especially for this purpose.
- The task requires collective input from highly specialised individuals.
- The task requires collective input and agreement from more than 20 people.
- The members of the team working on the task are in more than two locations.
- The success of the task is highly dependent on understanding the preferences or needs of individuals outside the group.
- The outcome of the task will be influenced by events that are highly uncertain and difficult to predict.
- The task must be completed under extreme time pressure.

5

Creating the future

The readings that follow emphasise the critical role that leaders play in the process of innovation. In market conditions where globally resourced companies have more or less the same access to resources, innovation becomes a potential differentiator and competitive weapon. Ask any Chief Executive whether they would like their business to be more innovative and they will say yes. But our experience tells us that this is as far as many organisations get – there are huge differences between the level of innovation practised across companies.

What is Innovation?

What is innovation? In the context of our readings innovation is the successful generation and implementation of new ideas in any aspect of the business. It may be a 'better thing to do' – product to make, business to enter, new procedure to implement, new concept of customer service and so on – or 'a better way to do it' – meaning improvements in operating approaches or interactions – that enhances the capability of the organisation to achieve its commercial goals. In short, companies that are innovative are able to conceive and bring to fruition novel and beneficial change in all aspects of their organisation.

There are three important aspects to this seemingly simple definition:

- Innovation is more than just product development.
- Innovation is not restricted to companies in growth businesses.
- Innovation is about 'different and better' not just 'different'.

Innovation in the way we are defining it is more likely to lead to better outcomes where it is a unique response or practice for the organisation, represents a break from past practice, is visible to others and has the potential to have a lasting impact. None of these implies that innovation has to encompass breakthrough thinking. Sometimes it will. But the majority of the time it will comprise incremental improvements over time arising from the kind of disciplined and structured process outlined in one or two of the readings.

What Best Practice Companies Do

The most innovative companies will make innovation a priority at Board level, releasing capital to support bold ideas wherever it is needed. They will continually examine where they should focus innovation effort for maximum benefit. They will trust empowered individuals to communicate and implement change in order to turn strategic aims into reality. They will, in other words, take a business approach to innovation.

The most impressive performance of the most innovative companies comes from a style that is more open than closely managed – hence the importance of climate and culture in some of the readings that follow. Specifically, they:

- Help people to interact with and understand the competitive environment they operate in (for example, when senior executives frequently visit customers and suppliers).
- Allow new ideas and knowledge to be shared, stored and freely accessed.
- Actively encourage diversity.
- Delay the premature evaluation of new ideas.

The most innovative bring their idea management processes to life by creating a working environment or climate that encourages ideas to flow. They:

- Promote and develop people who share a common set of values
- Reinforce management behaviours that encourage innovation
- Equip managers with the skills and knowledge that help them create a more favourable climate

Implications for Leaders

An effective balance between the roles of leaders and followers is crucial to sustaining an innovative working environment. This means setting a clear vision about the changes involved and working to get people's commitment to these. In the context of innovation it means neither over-managing nor under-managing – rather, as one CEO put it: 'applying a light hand to the tiller'. People need to know the boundaries of decision-making, need to be recognised and rewarded for challenging constructively traditional ways of working and selectively promoted where they have acted as effective role models at all levels in the organisation.

To be in the top innovation performance considerable drive and ambition is required. The starting point for any leader is to question and challenge her own assumptions and beliefs about innovation and then to act by:

- Searching for areas where innovation might transform the business.
- Pursuing the open style that engenders trust and therefore risk-taking.
- Raising the expectations of those who will deliver the agreed changes.
- Shaping the climate so that it is more receptive to innovation.
- Examining how new ideas are nurtured and harvested.
- Providing access across the organisation to ideas and knowledge.

Successful Innovators are Different

In a business setting, successful innovators are different from other people in that they develop new insights that define the problem or opportunity. This is the invention or creativity stage. Innovators are also able to implement their ideas by leading others in a way that maximises the odds of success. Finally, how much invention and implementation gets enacted is governed by the culture of the organisation as a whole and the climate of work units in particular.

In summary, we can think of innovation not just in terms of creativity around products and services but around a broader formula that applies to all aspects of a business:

INNOVATION = INVENTION + IMPLEMENTATION + CULTURE and CLIMATE

where INVENTION is fuelled by CREATIVITY, IMPLEMENT-ATION by LEADERSHIP and CULTURE and CLIMATE by the VALUES and BEHAVIOURS of leaders at every level in the organisation.

As Gary Hamel, the strategy guru, once remarked 'what we need are hierarchies of imagination rather than hierarchies of experience'. This could never be truer than now.

READING 24

Creating a climate for creativity and innovation

Goran Eckvall

Think about where you were the last time you had a really great idea or breakthrough for a challenge or problem you were facing. Can you describe the important characteristics or aspects of that situation? We often ask this question to groups of people and rarely hear their best ideas come while at work behind a desk, in front of their PCs or behind their Blackberries. When they begin to explain why their ideas seem to come better in one place than another they are talking about the **climate for creativity and innovation**.

Creativity and innovation need more than techniques. Tools, approaches and techniques are necessary but not sufficient. They need to be applied in a climate that is receptive to new ideas and ways of thinking. This **Reading** is about how such climates can be established.

Climate is different from culture. Culture concerns the values, beliefs, history, traditions etc. that reflect the deeper foundations of the organisation. The culture is long-standing, deeply rooted and usually slow to change. The organisation's climate however refers to the recurring patterns of behaviour exhibited in the day-to-day working environment. It is about 'how people feel about working here'. Culture, of course, affects climate as do several other factors such as leadership practices which is usually estimated as accounting for up to 65% of the variation in climate. Worth pondering on, that one.

Why does it matter? It matters because it's about figuring out ways 'to do more with less'. In other words how to 'grow the top line' while continually 'trimming the bottom line'. Without ideas or new ways of doing things the competitive gap will widen rather than narrow. As Gary Hamel the strategy guru remarked: "There is no such thing as *the* future. The future is not something that happens to you. The future is something you create." Creating such futures, according to Hamel, requires building 'hierarchies of imagination' rather than 'hierarchies of experience'.

The idea in brief – the 'core' idea

Building hierarchies of imagination – or climates for creativity and innovation in non-Hamel language – occupied the mind of Goran Ekvall a Swedish researcher active in the 1970s, 80s and 90s.

What Ekvall did as a result of studying 30 Swedish business organisations was to categorise these into *innovative, average and stagnated* based on people's perceptions of their working environment. Innovative, average and stagnated related to the organisation's development and successful commercial introduction of new products to the market. **Companies that were successful innovators based on hard business data scored more highly on specific climate dimensions than those that were average or stagnated.** This also held true in a wide range of non-Swedish companies across several business sectors.

So what are the climate dimensions that if established will help foster a climate for creativity and innovation?

The idea expanded – key findings

There are nine (although Ekvall started out with 10, two of which were later combined based on factor-analytic work by the **Creative Problem Solving Group***) and they are simple:

Challenge: *The degree to which people are involved in day-to-day operations, longer-term goals and strategies for achieving these.*

High levels of challenge and involvement mean that people are intrinsically motivated and committed to making contributions to the success of the organisation. The climate has a dynamic, electric and inspiring quality. People find meaningfulness in their work. As a result, they invest much energy. In the opposite situation, people are not engaged and feelings of indifference exist. The common sentiment and attitude are apathy and lack of interest.

Freedom: *The degree of independence and room for manoeuvre exhibited by people in the team.*

In a climate with much freedom, people are given autonomy to define much of their own work. People are able to exercise discretion in their day-to-day activities. People take the initiative to acquire and share information, make plans and decisions about their work. In the opposite climate, people work within strict guidelines and roles.

People carry out their work in prescribed ways with little room to redefine their tasks.

Trust: *The level of openness and degree of emotional safety in relationships.*

When there is a level of trust, individuals can be genuinely open and frank with each other. People can count on each other for personal support. People have a sincere respect for one another. Where trust is missing, people are suspicious of each other. As a result, they closely guard their ideas and themselves. People do not feel 'safe' in their working environment.

Idea Time: *The amount of time people use for developing new ideas.*

In the high idea-time situation, possibilities exist to discuss and test impulses and fresh suggestions that are not planned or included in the normal work. There are opportunities to take the time to explore and develop new ideas. Flexible timelines permit people to explore new avenues and alternatives. In the reverse case, every minute is booked and specified. The time pressure makes thinking outside of planned routines impossible. The goose lays many eggs but the quantity and quality deteriorate over time.

Playfulness: *The amount of humour, spontaneity and ease displayed in the workplace.*

A relaxed atmosphere where good-natured jokes and laughter occur often is indicative of this dimension. People can be seen having fun at work. The atmosphere is seen as easy-going and light-hearted.

The opposite climate is characterised by gravity and seriousness. The atmosphere is gloomy. Jokes and laughter are regarded as improper. Where there is laughter there is generally learning.

Conflict: *The presence of personal and emotional tensions in the team (in contrast to idea tensions – see Debates)*

When the level of conflict is high, individuals confront each other destructively. The climate is one of 'interpersonal warfare.' Plots, traps and territory struggles prevail. Gossip and backstabbing are the norm. In the opposite case, people behave in a maturer manner. People accept and deal effectively with differences and avoid personalising issues. Debate is robust but constructive because there is trust and openness.

Support: *The ways in which new ideas are treated.*

In the supportive climate ideas and suggestions are received in an attentive and professional manner. People listen to each other and encourage initiatives. Possibilities for trying out new ideas are created. The atmosphere is constructive and positive. When idea support is low, the automatic 'it won't work' prevails. Every suggestion is immediately refuted by a destructive counter-argument. Faultfinding and obstacle raising are typical responses.

Debates: *Active and robust encounters and disagreements between viewpoints, ideas and differing perspectives.*

In the innovative organisation many voices are heard and people are keen to put forward their ideas for consideration. People can often be seen voicing opposing opinions, disagreeing strongly and sharing a range of perspectives. Knowing you have been heard is more important than reaching a false consensus. Where debates are missing, people go along without any real commitment.

Risk-taking: The tolerance for uncertainty and ambiguity in the workplace.

Where there is risk-taking, bold new initiatives can be taken even when the outcomes are unknown. People feel as though they can take a gamble on some of their ideas. People will often 'go out on a limb' and be first to put an idea forward or give it a try. In a risk-avoiding climate there is a cautious, hesitant mentality. People err on the safe side. They like 'to sleep on it.' They set up committees and they cover their backsides.

The message is simple: **Organisations or teams that display these nine characteristics are more likely to develop new ideas and ways of doing things that are commercially beneficial than those that do not.**

* Adapted excerpts from original materials by CPSB and published with permission.

The idea in practice – putting the idea to work

The practical implications? What one thing can I implement a result of this research?

If you can put your hand on your heart and say 'the situation in which I work does not require and will not benefit from new ideas or ways of doing things' then stop reading here.

Otherwise, using the nine climate dimensions as backdrop, ask yourself (and maybe your colleagues):

1. What aspect of your working environment is MOST HELPFUL in supporting creativity and innovation?

2. What aspect of your working environment is LEAST HELPFUL in supporting creativity and innovation?

3. What is the MOST IMPORTANT ACTION you can take to improve the climate for innovation and creativity in your working environment?

Ekvall's work has been incorporated by **The Creative Problem Solving Group** into the Situational Outlook Questionnaire (SOQ) which provides a profile of an organisation's climate for creativity and innovation based on the perceptions of those who complete the instrument. To explore this and related materials go to www.cpsb.com/cnk/soq.html.

READING 25

How to become a management innovator

Gary Hamel

The author has long believed that innovation in leadership has been underplayed at the expense of the 'softer' aspects of management. When it as clear as a bell that the only way to *significantly* outperform the competition is to have and to implement different and better ideas it seems odd that little has really shifted in the world of management innovation. The guinea pig goes round faster and more efficiently but it still goes round.

It's taken a while for the strategy guru, Garry Hamel, to get to what really matters in management – that strategy cannot be separated from the people side of the business and people cannot be separated from innovation. In his *Harvard Business Review* article *The Why, What and How of Management Innovation* (February 2006 – permission gained from HBSP for this adapted excerpt), Hamel sets out his latest thoughts on management innovation with the usual freshness and challenge readers have come to expect from this thoughtful management thinker.

Reading 25 summarises the contents of this article.

The idea in brief – the 'core' idea

Management innovation is different from other kinds of innovation such as product innovation or business process reengineering. Hamel defines management innovation 'as a marked departure from traditional management principles, processes and practices or a departure from customary organisational forms that significantly alters the way the work of management is done. *Put simply, management innovation changes how managers do what they do.*'

And this potentially includes all managerial processes such as strategic planning, capital budgeting, project management, hiring and promotion, employee assessment, executive development and so on and so forth. His central theme is that the only way to change how managers work is to reinvent the processes that govern that work. While *operational innovation* focuses on a company's business processes *management innovation* targets a company's management processes.

The idea expanded – key findings

In most companies, Hamel argues, management innovation is ad hoc and incremental. Like Drucker before him Hamel believes that a systematic process for producing bold management breakthroughs must include four essential elements:

Element One – Commitment to a big management problem

In the same way as world-class teams need world-class problems the bigger and more soul stirring the problem the bigger the opportunity for innovation.

If you don't have or can't think of such problems then Hamel proposes three questions to help you:

Q1 What are the tough trade-offs that your company/activity never seems to get right? Your challenge is to find an opportunity to turn an 'either/or' into an 'and'.

Q2 What are big organisations bad at? Push yourself to imagine a company 'can't do' that you and your colleagues could turn into a 'can-do'.

Q3 What are the emerging challenges the future has in store for your business? If you scan the environment you are sure to see a tomorrow challenge that you should start tackling today.

Element Two – Search for new principles

Novel problems demand novel principles. Hand-me down principles will not do the job. Modern management practice is based on century old principles. The challenge is to uncover unconventional principles that open up new seams of management innovation. Two simple questions can help:

Q1 What things exhibit the attributes or capabilities that you'd like to build into your organisation?

Q2 What it is that imbues these exemplars with their enviable qualities?

New management principles such as variety, competition, allocation flexibility, devolution and activism (*although sounding somewhat Cameronian: Ed*) stand in marked contrast to those passed down from the Industrial Revolution. For example, many large organisations still resemble monarchies rather than democracies with political power concentrated in the hands of a few dozen senior executives and with little latitude for local experimentation. It's not that the old principles are wrong. They are just inadequate if the goal is strategic renewal. Companies such as IKEA, Apple, Pixar, Google are today's organisational models where there is little bureaucracy to drive out passion, ingenuity and self-direction. People bring their brains to work.

Element Three – Deconstruct management orthodoxies

What does this mean? It means loosening the grip that precedent has on your imagination. Painful as it may seem, a lot of what passes for management wisdom is unquestioned dogma masquerading as unquestionable truth. As commented in a previous MRU what is needed are 'hierarchies of imagination' rather than 'hierarchies of experience'.

As a management innovator Hamel argues that you must subject every management belief to two questions:

Q1 Is the belief toxic to the ultimate goal you are trying to achieve?

Q2 Can you imagine an alternative to the reality the belief reflects?

As old certainties crumble, the space for management innovation grows.

Element Four – Exploit the power of analogy

If the goal is to escape the straitjacket of conventional management wisdom it helps to study the practices of organisations that are decidedly unconventional.

Hamel cites a number. For example:

- Alcoholics Anonymous with 2m members and a HQ of 100
- Bangladesh's Grameen Bank which makes unsecured micro-loans to (largely female) five-person syndicates to start small businesses and which has 4m borrowers to date
- Google whose top team doesn't spend a lot of time cooking up grand strategies but works to create an environment that spawns lots of 'Googlets' that may one day grow into valuable new products and services.

The challenge is to hunt down equally unlikely analogies that suggest new ways of tackling thorny management problems. If you always do what you have always done you will always have what you have already got. Things will not move on.

The idea in practice – putting the idea to work

The practical implications? What one thing can I implement as a result of this research?

So how do we get the rubber on the road? What might we do now we are inspired, hopefully, to want to do something!

1. Discuss and agree with your colleagues (for example, in your leadership team) the single most important challenge for the future.
2. Identify the management process(es) that if changed might have a dramatic impact on this challenge.

3. Compile a list of probing questions that need to be answered for the management process(es) you have identified (for example: Who owns it? Who has the power to change it? Who are the customers? What do they think? And many more)
4. Assemble a cross-section of interested parties who might have a relevant (and possible irreverent) point of view. Get them to assess the process in terms of its impact on the management challenge identified earlier.
5. Empower the group to take action – either by reinventing the process or at least conducting low-risk trials that won't disrupt the entire organisation.

The goal is build a portfolio of *bold new management experiments* that have the power lift the performance of your company/activity ever higher than its peers.

So far, twenty-first century management isn't much different from twentieth-century management. Therein lies the opportunity. Take it!

READING 26

Breakthrough thinking from inside the box

Kevin P. Coyne, Patricia Gorman Clifford & Renee Dye

Consider the following:

"About 20 people – most of them chosen for political reasons – gather in a room. The leader is ether their boss, whose presence makes some people reluctant to offer what may be perceived as a silly idea, or a 'creativity facilitator' who neither understands the business nor thinks he should have to. Three pushy people dominate the session with their pet ideas while the others sit in silence. After the group is instructed to think outside the box ideas pop up randomly. Since 'there are no bad ideas' preposterous dreams consume much of the time and energy. Finally, because everyone knows you cannot force people to come up with good ideas, participants think it's OK to produce nothing – or not to follow up on anything the workshop did create".

Sound familiar?

So it did to Coyne, Clifford and Dye who set about researching how the most successful companies had reached their pre-eminent position discovering that in every case successes were built on breakthrough ideas that redefined the products and services in their markets. **But these ideas came less from 'thinking outside the box' and more from 'thinking inside the box'.**

Reading 26 summarises how *structured brainstorming* can generate a shower of great ideas that can be transformed into profitable reality (see *Harvard Business Review*, December 2007 – permission gained for this adapted excerpt – for a full account of the work).

The idea in brief – the 'core' idea

Coyne, Clifford and Dye propose **structured brainstorming** to focus people's minds in ways that spark fresh and relevant ideas.

167

They describe the approach as a middle way between the two extremes of boundless, unfettered ideas generation and highly structured quantitative analysis.

They argue that managers fail to generate a useable stream of ideas because they limit themselves to either of these approaches. They *either* encourage people to go wild and think outside the box or they assign them the task of cutting the old boxes (in the form of data) in new or different ways.

The problem with the first method is that most of us are not very good at unstructured, abstract brainstorming (the 'there are no bad ideas' approach) while the second method – slicing the data in new ways – almost invariably produces small to middling insights.

The solution, say the authors, is to embrace a two-part process: **posing powerful questions that unlock creativity and orchestrating the process for answering those questions.**

The best questions guide people to valuable – and often overlooked – corners of the universe of possible new ideas. It was a psychology professor (Mihaly Csikszentmihalyi) who studied how Nobel Laureates among others achieved breakthrough ideas, finding that once the right question had been crafted and asked, ideas flowed rapidly *(Ed: those of us involved in coaching know this to be true).*

More significantly, what mattered was not so much whether the question had been asked but **whether there was a question that *could* have uncovered the kind of extraordinary ideas that were produced.**

By examining over 50 breakthrough ideas across a spectrum of industries the researchers reverse engineered them to find the focused questions that could have led any intelligent manager to the same outcome. The 21 questions they identified are grouped into the following six categories:

- *Exploring unexpected successes* – e.g. who uses our product in ways we never expected or intended.
- *Examining binding constraints* – e.g. what's the biggest hassle of purchasing or using our product?
- Imagining perfection – e.g. how would our product change if it were customised for every customer?

- *De-averaging buyers and users* – e.g. who spends 50+% of our product cost to adapt it to their specific needs?
- *Revising assumptions about your processes and products* – e.g. which technologies embedded in our product have changed the most since the product was last redesigned?
- *Looking beyond your business boundaries* – e.g. what breakthroughs in efficiency/effectiveness have we made that could be applied in another industry?

Of potentially more use, however, is the scope for **developing your own list** by asking yourself every time you come across a new business idea that you think is really smart, '*What question would have caused me to see this opportunity first?*'

In other words, **learning to reverse engineer every great idea or innovation that you see will help to develop the kinds of questions that need to be asked if innovation in your own organisation is to flourish.**

Orchestrating the process

- **Put boundaries around the possible range of acceptable ideas then select and tailor the questions accordingly** – i.e. define the box within which people will do their thinking (you will need one question for every four participants every 30 minutes and maybe a 'killer' question that you give to every group).

- **Select participants who can produce original insights** – i.e. make sure there are enough people with the knowledge and information to contribute rather than people who are there for representative or political reasons (cast the net wide and deep).

- **Ensure that everyone is fully engaged** – i.e. get 100% of the participants to work at 100% of their capacity for 100% of the session (if this means using tricks such as offering glittering prizes for the best ideas that's fine too).

- **Structure the session to ensure social norms work for, not against you** – i.e. use small groups of four not one large group and put all the pushy people in the same group (the social norm in a group of 10 is for a only a few to speak out, the social norm for a group of four is for each person to speak out).

- **Focus every discussion using your pre-selected questions** – i.e. state the ground rules then allocate a single highly focused task for 20-30 minutes to each small group (so only one question is discussed and the best ideas reported back from each group's question-based discussion).

- **Don't rely solely on one brainstorming session** – i.e. do not restrict the process to a single event – schedule follow-up sessions or actions to ensure closure.

- **Narrow the list of ideas to the ones you will seriously investigate right away** – i.e. sort the ideas against pre-determined criteria before the session closes. If you don't, the chances are nothing will happen (a 20 person workshop produces about 20 ideas per hour so eight hours of idea generation means 150 ideas of which around 50 will be worthy of investigation).

The idea in practice – putting the idea to work

The practical implications? What one thing can I implement as a result of this research?

You

Look around you. This can be inside or outside your organisation. Identify what you consider to be a breakthrough idea. Now ask: *What question would have caused me to see this opportunity first?* Write it down. Now add two more similar questions of your own.

Team

Take an issue your team is grappling with. *Structure a session following the principles outlined above to generate ideas which if implemented will address the issue.* Be sure to spend time up-front crafting the questions to be used in the session.

Summary

Thinking inside the box by using semi-structured brainstorming runs counter to more traditional, freewheeling or strict quantitative approaches to idea generation. By following a two-stage method – asking the right questions and orchestrating the process – great ideas can be generated even in familiar settings. Nobel Laureates may do it naturally, the rest of us simply have to learn it.

READING 27

Leadership for innovation

Joanna Barsh, Marla M. Capozzi & Jonathan Davidson

The Creativity Research Unit of The Creative Problem Solving Group Inc. (CPSB) published this month the results of the their global survey (*Leadership for Innovation: A Global Climate Survey – A CRU Technical Report*) on the role leadership plays in creating a climate for innovation.*

Go to http://cpsb.com to learn more.

The results, following a coherent and rigorous research methodology, were based on a sample of 140 respondents from 103 different companies across 31 different industries.

Reading 27 encapsulates the 'top line' findings and practical implications of the survey results.

The idea in brief – the 'core' idea

The research explores the links between **Leadership Behaviour**, **Organisational Climate** and **Innovation** with organisational climate as the pivotal intervening variable.

Leadership -> **Organisational Climate** -> Innovation

We know that leaders influence innovation. We also know that climate is very different for organisations that are innovative versus those that are stagnated (see **Reading 24**: Creating a Climate for Creativity and Innovation).

What this study does, is tell us more about the effect of climate and the specific leadership behaviours that help or hinder innovation.

The research clearly confirmed that there is a strong relationship between leadership and innovation. Furthermore, **a leader must focus on the creation of a climate for creativity and innovation**

172

rather than on innovation directly in order to achieve the innovative outcomes desired.

The idea expanded – key findings

1a *The results show that a meaningful relationship exists between* **organisational climate** *and* **innovation in the work unit.**

Organisational climate is measured along nine dimensions:

- Challenge/involvement
- Freedom
- Trust/Openness
- Idea-time
- Playfulness/Humour
- Conflict (negatively correlated)
- Idea-Support
- Debate
- Risk-taking

With the exception of Conflict, the higher the climate scores on each of these dimensions the more successful innovation is likely to be. The lower the level of Conflict, the more successful innovation is likely to be.

Innovation in the work place was defined as success in implementing new ideas to obtain results.

1b *Using the same measures for organisational climate, the results show that a meaningful relationship exists between* **organisational** *climate* **and innovation in the organisation as a whole.**

2 *Respondents, who perceived their leader to be more effective, reported a significantly better organisational climate.*
This suggests that there is a meaningful relationship between the ways that individuals perceive their organisational

climate and how they observe their leader's ability to support innovation.

This confirms that leadership behaviours have a significant impact on the perceived organisational climate.

3 *The results show that there is a significant and meaningful correlation between **leadership** and both **work unit** and **organisation-wide innovation.***

However, when the influence of organisational climate is removed a decrease in the strength of the relationship occurs. This indicates that leadership effectiveness influences innovation to a large extent through organisational climate.

These outcomes clearly support the notion that organisational climate acts as an intervening variable between leadership behaviour and innovation both at work unit and organisational levels.

Leadership's role in establishing a climate for innovation is therefore reaffirmed.

So what specific behaviours do leaders need to demonstrate in order to help/hinder the creation of such a climate?

4 *The results show that eight macro-behavioural themes help or hinder innovation. Leaders **help** or **hinder** innovation by:*

- Controlling resource availability
- Delivering creativity and innovation training
- Fostering new ways of doing things
- Providing structure
- Sharing information
- Approaching mistakes and failures
- Including others in decision-making
- Focusing on priorities

Specific leader behaviours can be found that either help or hinder the creation of an organisational climate that supports innovation under each theme. For example, leaders can help innovation when they adjust deadlines and workload for novelty to occur ('Providing Structure').

In summary, leaders seeking to meet the innovation challenge must do so in large part by creating the work environment (climate) that supports creativity.

* Adapted from the original report and published with permission from CPSB.

The idea in practice – putting the idea to work

The practical implications? What one thing can I implement as a result of this research?

The practical implications of these findings are that leaders should focus on deliberately creating a climate for innovation instead of directly trying to influence their organisation's level of innovation by other means.

By adopting the right leadership practices (behaviours related to the eight themes above) an organisational climate (as measured by the nine factors above) will be created which fosters innovation at both work unit and organisation-wide levels.

How does your work unit climate rate on each of the nine factors? (Rate on a 1-10 scale)

What specific leadership behaviours related to the eight themes need to be developed to improve the ratings? (List one help and one hinder under each of the themes.)

READING 28

The role of corporate culture in radical innovation

Gerard J. Tellis, Jaideep C. Prabhu and Rajesh K. Chandy

Reading 28 synthesises the results of research carried out across 759 firms and 17 major economies of the world to determine the **key drivers of innovation**.

Radical innovation is an important driver of the growth, success and wealth of firms (and nations) and because of its importance researchers have proposed many theories about what drives innovation.

This rigorous study, conducted by Gerard J. Tellis, Jaideep C. Prabhu and Rajesh K. Chandy and published in the *Journal of Marketing* (January 2009), highlights the critical importance of corporate culture as a driver of radical innovation.

The idea in brief – the 'core' idea

Many theories have been proposed about what drives innovation both at firm and country levels. Key drivers have included government policy, labour, capital and national and corporate cultures. The authors contrast these theories with one based on the corporate culture of the firm and conclude that among the factors studied **corporate culture is the strongest driver of radical innovation across nations**.

Furthermore, the authors argue that **the commercialisation of radical innovations translates into a firm's financial performance**. In fact, it is identified as a stronger predictor of financial performance than other popular measures such as patents.

The authors discuss the implications of these findings for both research and practice.

The idea expanded – key findings

Corporate culture refers to a core set of attitudes and practices that are shared by the members of the firm.

In this research, the authors identify three firm level attitudes and three firm level practices that may drive innovation:

Firm level attitudes

- **Willingness to cannibalise assets** – being willing to sacrifice current profit-generating assets so that work can proceed on the next generation of innovations.
- **A future orientation** – realising the limitations of current technology and the emergence of a new generation of technology that may become dominant in the future.
- **Tolerance for risk** – fostering and promoting a tolerance for risk that allows a trade-off to be made between a current and future uncertain stream of profits.

Firm level practices

Three practices were identified that engender and sustain the three firm level attitudes described above:

- **Empowerment of product champions** – empowering an individual with the resources to explore, research and build on promising but uncertain, future technologies.
- **Establishing incentives for enterprise** – refraining from rewarding only or primarily senior management of current products as opposed to ensuring adequate incentives for employees who venture to explore or build new enterprises for the firm.
- **Creation and maintenance of internal markets** – (i) creating internal autonomy – the extent to which decision-making authority is devolved (ii) creating internal competition – allowing divisions or groups within the firm to compete among themselves to identify promising technologies and build innovations.

The research findings show that most of the traditional variables have little effect on radical innovation once corporate culture is accounted for. **Internal corporate culture is a very important driver of radical innovation.** All of the above factors (except internal markets) have significant effects.

The authors quote examples to illustrate the unique role played by corporate culture:

A traditional innovative country such as the US can be home to innovative firms such as **Apple** or **FedEx** as well as lumbering ones such as **Kodak** and **Kmart**.

Innovative firms such as **Samsung** (Korea) and **Infosys** (India) in traditional lagging economies can leapfrog slumbering giants in traditionally advanced economies.

Thus, corporate culture, the authors deduce, seems more important than traditional country drivers in predicting radical innovation in firms across nations. **Innovative firms are similar – they share the same cultural practices and attitudes despite differences in geography.**

Radical innovations also translate into financial value to the firm. Market-to-book value is significantly increased even after controlling for the effects of patents, R&D and other variables. Patents are not as important in influencing financial value as are radical innovations in firms (for example, Apple with a little over 100 patents stole Sony's market for mobile music while Sony with thousands of patents refrained from cannibalising its successful Walkman and music business).

In summary, the research questions some long held premises about radical innovation and demonstrates the key role played by an individual firm's culture that is primarily shaped by its founders, its history and above all else its leaders.

The idea in practice – putting the idea to work

The practical implications? What one thing can I implement as a result of this research?

Managers can be attuned to the cultural factors referred to above, measure them and foster them to maintain a culture of relentless innovation.

Hold your firm's culture up to the mirror:

Using our well-known 1-10 scale (1=Low/10-=High) to what extent would you describe your firm's culture as innovative?

Where does it stand in terms of the three attitudes?

- Willingness to cannibalise assets
- A future orientation
- Tolerance for risk

Using the same 1-10 scale, to what extent does your firm:

- Empower product champions
- Establish incentives for enterprise
- Create internal markets and competition?

Bearing in mind **Readings 24 & 25** what effect does this culture have on the climate of your activity? What might you do to offset this? (Think: Management Practices).

6

Making Things Happen

In Chapter 2 we positioned Execution as the third segment of our EOL (Effective Organisational Leadership) framework and described it as the discipline that focuses the organisation's ideas and energy to getting things done.

Execution capability is primarily a function of strong management. In the days before leadership became the hot topic it now is, students of business administration would be taught to think in terms of planning, organising and controlling. But as thinking about leadership developed, particularly the transformational aspects of leadership, management as a discipline in its own right became sidelined. Leadership became sexy. It was good to be a leader, not so good to be a manager. Managers, according to Steve Jobs at Apple, were simply 'bozos'. Leadership and management lost their mutual connection. If you had to be one or the other it was better to be a leader.

Leadership grew in momentum chiefly because of the accelerated rate of change that took place in markets, in particular globalisation and the forces that shaped this. As Peter Drucker was fond of saying: 'Some time in the 1980s the world shifted from stability to turbulence'. Leadership was required to ensure that organisations coped with and managed the level of turbulence they faced.

But change did not replace complexity. As John Kotter in his many books has pointed out, change coupled with complexity needs both leadership and management. Large, complex, global organisations need both strong leadership and strong management. In the development of our EOL Framework (see Chapter 2) this was recognised by making execution, or management, an integral part of the leadership framework. The precise combination of leadership and management would be situationally determined but it was as important for organisations not to be over-managed and under-led as it was for them to be over-led and under-managed. Unfortunately, the idea of being over-managed and under-led had a certain popular appeal which in turn led to management playing 'second fiddle'. Being strategic and visionary mattered more than simply 'getting things done'.

Management is an integral part of leadership. Drucker recognised this: "Effective executives develop action plans. Executives are doers. They execute. Effective executives define desired results by asking 'what contributions should the business expect from them over the next 18 months to two years?' What results will they commit to? With what deadlines?"

Doers are the people who energise people, are decisive on tough issues, get things done through others and follow through as second nature. They are natural and relentless performance managers and builders of capability. They are coaches rather than micro-managers but place equal emphasis on challenging and supporting those they manage.

It is worth the reader skipping back to **Reading 11** (Chapter 3). There we listed the nine factors that research showed had the greatest impact on performance. Take a pencil and put a tick against each of the factors where you believe this is something a good coach will do. Coaching is the centrepiece of performance management. By targeting research-led practices, the manager-as-coach can be more laser-like in managing employees' performance.

In the same way that leaders' visions are shaped by the broader strategy of the business and levels of commitment by the organisation's culture the broader structures and systems of the organisation influence execution-related behaviours. To the extent that a leader's vision or a new strategy requires significantly different behaviours from those that were appropriate in the past, management tools and broader planning and control systems may require significant modification to facilitate implementation.

Nowhere could this be truer than in the performance and reward structures a company engages in. People will deliver what they are rewarded for, even where this may not be in the best long-term interests of the business (a practice well highlighted in the 2008 credit crunch where deal volumes and short-term profitability were rewarded more highly than future return to shareholders). Many financial institutions appear to have undergone leadership bypass surgery in the run up to the 2008-credit crunch and 2009 deep recession.

There is a final issue to address in this chapter on 'Making Things Happen'. It is true to say that some personality types will be more execution-minded than others. It is as much in their DNA as it is for others to be strategic-minded or people-minded. The highly focused, structured, practical thinking type who is task-driven with a high need for closure is more likely to get things done than some of their more flexible, easy-going counterparts. Or so it would seem. Over many years of coaching such task-driven, largely alpha males we have learnt that this focus on results often back fires. Because such individuals are more likely to have a blind spot around interpersonal relations they are less likely to gain the commitment required of others and therefore fail in their quest for execution. As for all things in life, there is something to be said for balance.

In the readings that follow, inspiration is provided by one of the greatest businessmen in the UK, the late Sir John Harvey-Jones who learnt it 'the hard way'. It is worth remembering that his book, Making it Happen, was published six years after Tom Peter's In Search of Excellence stormed the management world. While the latter, with its emphasis on culture, became almost cult reading, the former, with its emphasis on execution, did not. It is a matter of debate as to which book contained the most enduring lessons for practising managers.

READING 29

Making it happen

John Harvey-Jones

2008 witnessed the loss of two giants: one, Sir Edmund Hillary from the world of mountaineering, the other Sir John Harvey-Jones from the world of business.

For readers who maybe too young to remember, John Harvey-Jones became Chairman of ICI in 1982 when the company made losses of £16 million. Two years later, ICI became the first British company to make pre-tax profits in excess of £1 billion.

His book *Making it Happen* (1988)* looked back at his years at the helm of ICI. **Reading 29** celebrates his life by providing one or two quotations from each of the chapters of a book written by someone 'who did it'.

The idea in brief – the 'core' idea

John Harvey-Jones became chairman at a critical time in the company's history. By cutting manning levels and investing in plant he solved the problem of overproduction with low productivity. The workforce was cut by a third in five years and profits per employee more than doubled. He also looked for new opportunities and reduced the company's reliance on cyclical commodities.

More significantly, however, he changed the style of management, cutting bureaucracy, shortening lines of communication and removing status barriers. He also emphasised the need to turn ingenious ideas into marketable products.

Dressed more like a thespian than a businessman, Harvey-Jones was not afraid of change being one of that breed of businessman who expect the world to look different every week. In three years he bought and sold 63 companies for ICI and was offered 460 part-time jobs (of which he accepted 39) when he stepped down.

The idea expanded – key findings

Making it Happen

- "Plainly, in any large enterprise the boss cannot be directly involved in everything and some means have to be found to transfer his belief and commitment to others."
- "Management is not about the preservation of the status quo. It is about maintaining the highest rate of change that the organisation and the people within it can stand."
- "I believe absolutely that in the future it will be the company that conforms to the individual that will attract and motivate the best people."
- "Each one of us has to develop our own style and our own approach, using such skills and personal qualities as we have inherited."
- "One of the lessons I have learnt in life is that a bit more time thinking and planning will immeasurably increase the effectiveness of one's input."

Setting the Direction

- "The business that is not being purposefully led in a clear direction which is understood by its people is not going to survive and all of history shows that this is the case."
- "There is no point in deciding where your business is going until you have actually decided with great clarity where you are now."
- "In deciding where you would like the business to be, you need a great deal of discussion and new thinking. The idea of doing this through a planning department or through a paper on strategy presented to the Board seems to me to be quite inadequate. The process involves large amounts of time and constant discussion with those involved lower down the line who will actually execute the strategies on which the future depends."
- "Very frequently people closer to the marketplace than to the Board are more realistic about the possibilities than those at the top."

Switching On or Switching Off?

- "In deciding where we should go we have to transfer ownership of the direction by involving everyone in the decision. 'Making it happen' means involving the hearts and minds of those who have to execute and deliver. It cannot be said often enough that these are not the people at the top of the organisation but those at the bottom."

The How

- "In my philosophy of management it follows that if the strategic objective has been worked out and agreed, and the right conditions have been created in which people can be switched on, the 'how' of what is to be achieved is a matter for delegation."
- "We businessmen are an international race of little wind-up, instant action men and indeed so anxious are we for achievement that we are often well down the road on an inadequately thought-out basis while others, more prudent than we, have stopped to think."

All Change

- "The management of change in every country involves similar problems and requires similar approaches. The differences relate more to the stage at which people begin to worry and at which the climate is conducive to change."
- "I do not believe in the myth of the great leader who can suddenly engender in his people a vision and lead them to an entirely new world."
- "While it is true that it is very difficult to lead change against the grain of the feelings of the people in your business, it is fatal to wait until those feelings have developed into a head of steam. The art is to discern the direction of the feelings and to instigate change before everyone is so frustrated and dissatisfied that they are boiling for revolution."
- "People who work for organisations like my own where the account books are open and where every man or woman knows

whether we are doing well or badly and knows the nature of the problems, are much quicker to recognise the need for change than those who are kept in ignorance."

Catalysts and Judo

- "I have always believed that small interventions, carefully thought out, can have an effect far out of proportion to the amount of effort involved in the actual intervention."
- "The lines between manipulation, management and leadership are fine, but devastatingly clear in the minds of individuals. Manipulation, or the fear of it, arouses more antagonism and is more antipathetic to business success than almost anything else, and yet the really skilful manager has to take actions which can lead to such accusations."

Boardmanship

- "There are almost as many theories of management as there are managers and of course this is the problem. Each one of us has to develop our own personal management style that suits us and the people with whom we are working."

The Emperor's Clothes

- "If the change from being a manager to being an executive director is a big and traumatic one, there is little doubt in my personal experience that the task of becoming a non-executive director is the biggest learning experience of all."
- "The most frustrating situation of all is for the non-executive director who is aware either that there is no strategy or that the strategy being pursued is inadequate and yet he cannot succeed in persuading or leading or teaching the executive team to work out something realistic despite the fact that this is one of his major responsibilities and roles."

The Top Job

- "It is only when you become aware of the range, scope and

incredible responsibility of the job that you realise that there is almost limitless opportunity to be ineffective unless you are totally clear about how you are going to set about it."

- "You must be clear in your own mind that there is no way that one man can manage an enormous company. The job of the chairman or CEO is to manage his colleagues on the Board and to manage the company through the Board."

- "The only job in the entire company where it is totally clear where the added value lies is probably that of the Chairman or CEO."

Board Work

- "When I took over as chairman one of my first actions was to arrange for the executive directors and myself to spend a week away together in order to discuss how the Board should lead the company and how we should organise our work."

The 'U' Factor

- "There cannot be anybody who has held a senior position who is not plagued with continued self-doubt. The more confident the external appearance, the more likely the individual is to torment himself privately with questions as to whether the achievement is enough, the commitment is enough, the certainty is enough or the risk is too great or too small."

- "I have often said that the prime characteristic that I have detected in top leaders is mental and physical toughness."

- "Eventually you rely on your ideals and the picture in your mind of the sort of person you would like to be and would like to remain. I think it necessary to have this idealistic portrait to which you aspire tucked away where you can check up to see how you are altering."

And So to Tomorrow

- "Anyone reading this book will have realised by now that there are two aspects of business: one is people and the other is change.

Without change nothing is possible. Not to change is a sure sign of imminent extinction."

- "Business is, and always has been, about people."

The idea in practice – putting the idea to work

The practical implications? What one thing can I implement as a result of this research?

Making it Happen contained John Harvey-Jones's personal **reflections on leadership**.

What are yours?

READING 30

The secrets of getting people to say 'yes'

Robert B. Cialdini

In October last year the *Sunday Times* reported success in a little known company: The Solvay Pharmaceuticals and Healthcare Company. In one day it had increased the number of units of flu vaccines sold from 6,000 to 20,000.

The apparent foundations of this success were the simple application of the principles summarised in this **Reading**, derived from the best-selling book *Influence: Science and Practice* by Robert B Cialdini published by Allyn & Bacon (2001). *

The book examines the process that causes humans to change and is based on three years research during which Cialdini went underground as a participant observer working in petrol stations, cafes, estate agents and suchlike to gather scientific evidence on 'how, why and when people say yes'.

The idea in brief – the 'core' idea

Although there are probably thousands of different tactics to influence people the core idea expanded in the book is that the majority fall within six basic categories. Each of these categories is governed by a fundamental psychological principle that directs human behaviour and, in so doing, gives the tactics their power.

The findings of the research are organised around these six key principles each of which can be used by practitioners who need the other party 'to say yes'. Each principle is examined as to its ability to produce a distinct type of agreement, that is an **automatic willingness** 'to say yes' without thinking first: a trend that the ever-accelerating pace and crush of our electronic and media-driven world will make more prevalent in the future.

Much of the agreement reaching process (where person A is

189

influenced to accede to person B's request) can be understood says Cialdini, in terms of the human tendency for **automatic, short cut responding**. Most people have developed a set of trigger features for when to say 'yes'. Each of these trigger features can be used like a 'weapon of influence' to stimulate people to agree to requests.

So what are these six 'weapons of influence'?

The idea expanded – key findings

1 The Principle of Reciprocation

This rule says that we should try to repay in kind what another person has provided. If a person does us a favour we should do one in return. If a couple invite you to a dinner party then you invite them back in return.

By virtue of the reciprocity rule we feel **obliged to repay**. This sense of future obligation makes possible the development of various kinds of continuing relationships and transactions.

So in a commercial setting, the tactic of giving something before asking for a return favour can lead to a profitable transaction.

Another way of achieving the same end is for the individual to make an initial concession that stimulates a return concession. By starting with an extreme request that is sure to be rejected a requester can then profitably retreat to a smaller request (the one that was desired all along) which is likely to be accepted because it appears to be a concession.

2 The Principle of Commitment and Consistency

This rule is based on our desire to be (and to appear) consistent with what we have already done. **Once we make a choice or take a stand we will encounter personal and interpersonal pressure to behave consistently with that commitment.** Those pressures will cause us to respond in ways that justify our earlier decision.

Securing an initial commitment from the other person is the key. After making the commitment the other person is more likely to agree to requests (i.e. say 'yes') that reflect their prior commitment.

Commitments are most effective when they are *formalised, visible and self-generated.* So a commitment that is made public and written down is more likely to generate consistent responses in the future than a commitment that is left unspoken or assumed.

3 The Principle of Social Proof

This states that we determine what is correct by finding out what other people think is correct. **We view a behaviour as correct in a given situation to the degree that we see others performing it.** The actions of those around us will act as important guides.

In a commercial setting the principle can be used to get a person 'to say yes' by informing the person that referenced individuals (the more the better) have already said 'yes'. Powerful imitative effects have been found across a wide cross-section of business and non-business situations.

Social proof is most potent under two conditions. First, *uncertainty.* When people are unsure, or when a situation is ambiguous, they are more likely to be influenced by others. Secondly, *similarity.* People are more inclined to follow the lead of similar others. The more people are perceived to be 'like you' the more likely will their behaviours be replicated.

4 The Principle of Liking

We most prefer to say 'yes' to the requests of people we know and like (think: Tupperware parties).

A number of features will influence overall liking:

- The **physical attractiveness** of the other person – attractive people are more persuasive both in terms of getting what they request and in changing others' attitudes.
- **Similarity.** As stated above, we like people who are like us, and we are more willing to 'say yes' to their requests, often in an unthinking manner.
- **Familiarity** through repeated contact with a person is another factor that facilitates liking and therefore agreement especially

when the circumstances are positive and there is *mutual and successful co-operation.*

- Another factor linked to liking is **association**. Forming a connection between yourself or your product/service with something positive/favourable will increase your influence (as many sports celebrities and product advertisers well know).

5 The Principle of Authority

People defer to experts. **Acting contrary to their interests, many normal, psychologically healthy people will be influenced by the perceived expert, the authority figure.** Many studies have shown this to be the case.

Deference to authorities can occur in a mindless fashion, as a kind of *decision-making shortcut.* This is especially true where the authority figure possesses genuine, high levels of expertise.

When reacting to authority in such as automatic fashion there is a tendency to do so in response to *the symbols rather than the substance of the authority.*

Three kinds of symbols have been shown to be influential:

- Titles
- Clothing
- Automobiles

In separate studies investigating the influence of each of these symbols, individuals possessing one or another of them were accorded more deference or obedience.

6 The Principle of Scarcity

According to the scarcity principle, **opportunities seem more valuable to us when they are less available**. (Think: answering a telephone call in the middle of a face-to-face conversation). In commercial settings 'limited number offers' or 'deadline tactics' are examples.

The scarcity principle holds for two reasons: first, because things that are difficult to attain are typically more valuable, *their availability acts as a shortcut cue to its quality.* Secondly, as things become less available we lose freedoms. *We respond to the loss of freedoms by wanting to have them more than before.* The principle applies equally to information (for example, limiting access to a message causes individuals to want to receive it more).

The scarcity principle is especially potent under two conditions: first, scarce items are heightened in value when they are *newly scarce* – i.e. when they have become recently restricted. Secondly, when we have to *compete with others* for whatever is scarce (think: petrol queues).

Concluding Thought (Instant Influence)

The changing form and accelerating pace of modern life is changing the way we make decisions. Although we perhaps want to make thoughtful, considered decisions more and more we are forced into a shortcut approach in which 'saying yes' is made on the basis of a single, usually reliable piece of information.

The most popular and reliable triggers for agreement according to this research are the six categories outlined above. **Individuals who are in roles where 'getting a yes' is critical are more likely to be successful if they infuse their requests with one or another of the six triggers of influence.**

Such triggers only become exploitative when they are not a natural feature of the situation but are fabricated by the practitioner concerned. Such fabrication should be opposed in all cases.

*Caldini, INFLUENCE: SCIENCE & PRACTICE, © 2009, 2000 Pearson Education, Inc Reproduced by permission of Pearson Education, Inc.

The idea in practice – putting the idea to work

The practical implications? What one thing can I implement as a result of this research?

- Think of a recent situation where 'getting a yes' was important for you but you failed or you found the experience difficult. Embed the situation firmly in your mind and recall the steps you went through as accurately as possible (write them down).

- Now review the six principles above. Which one (or more) of these lends itself most readily to the situation you have in mind? Why?
- Replay the situation using the principle you have selected. Do you feel a more successful outcome would have been achieved had you applied this principle originally?
- If you do, identify an upcoming situation where 'getting a yes' matters. Identify the principle(s) you will use in your discussion. Script the scene, rehearse it with a colleague and then apply it to the real situation.

READING 31

Doing what's obvious but not easy

David Maister

Many of us will have made our New Year resolutions. Few of us will see them through. Why?

This is the subject addressed by David Maister (the professional services firm guru and best-selling author of books such as The Trusted Adviser and Managing the Professional Services Firm) in his latest book **Strategy and the Fat Smoker.***

The title comes from Maister's headline article about a fat smoker who knows that to become healthier s/he should probably lose weight and stop smoking. But s/he doesn't. Why not?

The reasons are the same whether it's New Year Resolutions, losing weight/stopping smoking or achieving our strategic goals in business. We know *what* to do, we know *why* we should do it and we probably know *how* to do it.

Yet we don't change – most of us – as individuals or as businesses. **Reading 31** distils the key points from Maister's book drawing on materials provided by ChangeThis (see the website http://changethis.com/content/reader).

The idea in brief – the 'core' idea

The primary reason why we don't change is because **the rewards and pleasures are in the future while the disruption, discomfort and discipline needed to get there are in the present.**

To implement our strategy, achieve our goals we have to change our habits *now*. Then we have to *sustain* the new habits. Then we get the benefits.

If you're not willing to make the changes that a specific goal requires it doesn't matter how important that goal is. In strategic planning for example, the necessary outcome is not *analytical insight* but *resolve*.

The core questions are: Which of our (personal/business) habits are we *really* prepared to change? Which lifestyle changes are we *really* prepared to make? What issues are we *really* ready and prepared to tackle head-on?

While discussing strategy is stimulating and intellectually energising, discussing what you are prepared to accept and do to implement the strategy (or achieve a goal) is something different.

Maister poses the following questions:

- Which diet, if integrated into the normal running of the firm, would actually get us to where we want to be?
- Which diet would we be prepared to adopt as a central part of our lifestyle?
- If we don't like any of the diets suggested can we think of another that will be as powerful but that we could live with more easily?

If there is no specific diet that all your people can agree to follow then you must conclude that you are not really willing or able to pursue that strategic goal. You don't have to strive for excellence if you are not willing to do what it takes to achieve it. Just being competent is an option.

The idea expanded – key findings

Maister identifies six things about getting people to change without the threat of crisis (be it a heart attack or the business equivalent):

Accept that it's about a permanent change in lifestyle

- Avoid thinking about improvement/change (and strategy) as being a distinct schedule of activities separate from regular business activities (i.e. there is real life and there is the diet). *Make the diet part of the normal, daily routine.*

Change the way the way progress is measured

- Strategy, if it is to be lived and achieved, is about modifying the very rules of daily living and scorekeeping, so inventing *new ways of publishing and disseminating tracking measures is critical.*

   "Once a quarter the CEO emails all active clients with a request to click on one of three buttons: green if they are satisfied, amber if they have concerns and red if they are unhappy. The CEO reviews all the replies following up on every one that is not green. Every quarter the results are published to everyone in the firm. Even the mail clerks can see how satisfied the clients are."

Leadership: Get serious or get out of the way

- The single biggest difficulty in getting an organisation to stick to its diet is convincing the members that *top management really wants them* to (if top management are ambiguous about whether they want premium priced business resulting from a differentiated strategy versus lower margin but secure business then members are unlikely to engage in the kind of strategic behaviours desired).

- If top management want people to believe a new strategy is being followed they must figure out a way for it to be *credible* that they, top management have changed their thinking and are prepared to change the way *they* act, measure and reward.

- A large part of really bringing about strategic change is designing some action, a new system that visibly, inescapably and irreversibly *commits* top management to the strategy.

Principles are more effective than tactics

- Where the diet (e.g. strategic rules) achieves the force of *moral principle* the odds are significantly higher that successful implementation will be achieved.

- Managers who get things done – see things through – are those who tend to have an *ideology* – their people know that they believe in something (think McKinsey, Goldman Sachs, Bain)

People must volunteer

- Change, or the pursuit of a challenging goal, only really works when the individual is doing it for him/herself and has made a *personal choice* to do it. Doing it because others want it or expect it doesn't work. The motivation needs to be intrinsic. Will is more important than technique.

- To achieve any goal you must really *want* the goal. It is dangerous to assume that everyone wants the same goal with the same level of intensity. Not everyone is prepared to do what it takes for other people's wants.

- Execution is *hard work*. So it needs to be hard work that a person loves to do. No one can instil passion in someone else. It has to come from within. Duty and obligation by themselves are a low-grade fuel. Must-win battles require Must-win commitment.

People must get on or off the bus

- For a business organisation that excels, strategy cannot be what 'most of us do most of the time'. *Individuals have to make a choice.*

- Strategy making and execution is often about getting some senior people to leave and bringing some new people in (what Jim Collins in Good to Great called 'getting the right people on and off the bus'). There is always an 'opt in' and an 'opt out' choice – *silent dissenters need to decide.*

- Everyone in the business has to decide if they want to try hard enough. They may do so if they believe the effort is serious. *They won't if they see an undecided or uncommitted team at the top.*

* Originally self-published. Now available through Spangle Press © 2008. Adapted excerpts by permission of the author.

The idea in practice – putting the idea to work

- The practical implications? What one thing can I implement as a result of this research?

- Once we know the diet there is a need for **skilled coaching** to lead individuals and teams through the struggle to attain the goals they have committed to. Be the best coach you can.

- The primary aim at the beginning of a change – whether it's personal or business – is to **get people to believe that it is doable** and that all that is being asked is that they try. This means early successes that can be built on.

- Talking about the **'next small' step** in the context of principles therefore makes sense as does celebrating each small accomplishment ('as long as you are trying and improving you are one of us').

- Provide **lots of encouragement**. We all need to play mind games with ourselves when we struggle to achieve goals and build new habits into our life. If you can make a game of something it helps to sustain the effort.

- **Make standards of behaviour explicit** so that both the manager and employee know when there is a gap. Model and reward the desired behaviours.

NOW:

If you haven't already, look to next year and identify one core goal (personal or business) that you really want to achieve and which will impact considerably on you as a person or on the business in which you work.

WHAT DO YOU NEED TO DO TO ENSURE THAT YOU WILL SEE THIS THROUGH TO COMPLETION?

READING 32

Execution: the discipline of getting things done

Larry Bossidy & Ram Charan

Think of a famous company. One that became a benchmark for its industry and then slipped became 'second-best'. The chances are that such slippage reflected a failure in Execution. **Reading 32** summarises the highly practical thoughts and experiences of Larry Bossidy (ex-CEO of Allied Signal) and business consultant, Ram Charan, in their thought-provoking book *Execution: The Discipline of Getting Things Done* (published with permission from Random House Business Books), a standard text for Harvard Business School students.

The idea in brief – the 'core' idea

Execution is a discipline. It is the job of the business leader and has to be 'in the culture'. But it too often gets neglected because to put it bluntly it's not seen to be as sexy as some other business functions such as strategy. So to understand execution you have to keep three key points in mind:

- Execution is a discipline that is integral to strategy.
- Execution is the major job of the business leader.
- Execution is a core element of an organisation's culture.

The discipline of execution is based on a set of building blocks that leaders must use to operate effectively three core processes: **the People Process, the Strategy Process** and **the Operations Process**.

The idea expanded – key findings
So what are these building blocks of execution?

Building Block One: The Leaders' Seven Essential Behaviours

- Know your people and your business.
- Insist on realism.
- Set clear goals and priorities.
- Follow-through.
- Reward the doers.
- Expand people's capabilities.
- Know yourself.

Building Block Two: Creating the Framework for Cultural Change

Cultural change gets real when the aim is execution. Peoples' behaviours need to change so that they produce results. "First you tell people clearly what results you are looking for. Then you discuss with them how to get those results as a key element in the coaching process. Then you reward people for delivering. If they fall short you provide additional coaching, withdraw rewards, give them other jobs or let them go. When you do these things you create a culture of getting things done (P86)."

The framework has to be **operationalised**. This means focusing on changing people's beliefs rather than the company's core values. Behaviours are beliefs turned into action.

The foundation of changing behaviour is **linking rewards to performance** and making the linkages transparent. If a company rewards and promotes people for execution, its culture will change.

You cannot have an execution culture without **robust dialogue**. Robust dialogue starts when people go in with open minds and feel they can speak candidly. Informality is critical to candour. And robust dialogue always ends with closure – people agree about what each person has to do and when. The key is that people act their way to thinking rather than think their way into acting because they are

201

driven for results.

Finally leaders get the behaviour they exhibit. **The culture of a company is the behaviour of its leaders.** You change the culture of a company by changing the behaviours of its leaders. You measure the change in culture by measuring the change in the personal behaviour of its leaders and the performance of the business.

Building Block Three: Having the Right People in the Right Place

Why aren't the right people in the right jobs? Obviously, they should be.

- **Lack of knowledge** – the job has not been defined in terms of its three or four non-negotiable criteria – i.e. things the person *must* do in order to succeed
- **Lack of courage** – the manager does not have the emotional wherewithal to confront the employee when required
- **Psychological comfort** – the leaders who promote the wrong people simply feel comfortable with them. In other words, loyalty based on the wrong reasons

All the above reflect one absolutely fundamental shortcoming – **lack of personal commitment and deep engagement in the People Process.**

What kind of people are you looking for?

Too often, senior people get seduced by the educational and intellectual qualities of the candidate. They fail to ask: how good is this person at getting things done? Is s/he a doer?

Doers are the people who:

- Energise people.
- Are decisive on tough issues.
- Get things done through others.
- Follow through as second nature.

It's essential to get to the essentials of what makes the person effective. Effective means excelling both at WHAT has been achieved and HOW it has been achieved. Meeting commitments the wrong way can do enormous damage to a business.

The three building blocks described above provide the foundation for the three core processes of execution. **If you have leaders with the right behaviours, a culture that rewards execution and a consistent system for the right people in the right jobs, the foundation is in place for operating each of the three core processes.**

Core Process One: the People Process

- Provides linkage to the strategic plan and its near (0-2 years). Medium (2-5 years) and long-term milestones and the operating plan targets including specific financial targets.
- Developing the leadership pipeline through continuous improvement, succession depth and reducing retention risk.
- Deciding what to do about non-performers.
- Transforming the mission and operations of the HR function.

Core Process Two: the Strategy Process

- Defines a business's direction and positions it to move in that direction.
- Devotes the utmost attention to the how's of executing the strategy.
- Represents an action plan that business leaders can rely on to reach their business objectives.
- Is linked to the People Process to ensure the right people are in place to execute the strategy.

Core Process Three: the Operations Process

- Allows a budget to be speedily and efficiently built with involvement of the key players.
- Is based on sound assumptions arising from robust debate.
- Provides a framework for producing the operating plan: setting the targets, agreeing the action plans and identifying follow-

through measures.
- Incorporates mechanisms for agreeing trade-offs.

The heart of the working of a business is how the three processes link together. Leaders need to master each process and the way they work together as a whole.

The discipline of execution is based on a set of building blocks that every leader must use to design, install and operate effectively the three core processes outlined above.

The idea in practice – putting the idea to work

The practical implications? What one thing can I implement as a result of this research?

First, answer two key questions:

1. To what extent does your organisation demonstrate personal commitment and deep engagement in the People Process?
2. To what extent does your organisation have a Culture of Execution?

Now answer the following:

3. To what extent do leaders in your organisation display the seven essential behaviours? Which are the strongest/weakest?
4. To what extent do *you* display the seven essential behaviours? Which are the strongest/weakest?
5. Is there any overlap between your answers to Q3 and Q4? If so, what might this imply?

Finally, what single action could *you* take to make your organisation more execution orientated?

READING 33

Getting control of your life

David Allen

Reading **33** summarised a corporate approach to 'getting things done'. In this reading, we stick with the same topic but focus on 'getting things done' at the individual level. A corporate approach is fine but unless individuals stay focused and organised nothing will happen. The very best thinking on this subject – in our view – comes from the research and practice of David Allen who the author learned about when undertaking consulting work for one of the remaining investment banks that has so far remained independent without government funding. To do justice to his work, the book to read is *Getting Things Done* by David Allen, published by Judy Piatkus (Publishers) Limited (2001).

The idea in brief – the 'core' idea

The process at the core of David Allen's work around mastering workflow is his five-stage model: (1) *collect* (2) *process* (3) *organise* (4) *review* (5) *do*. While this may seem high level it incorporates everything that has our attention at any time in any context. The added value lies in Allen's ability to convert this framework into a robust, practical approach that works. **The mistake that most people make is when they try to do all five phases at one time.**

So let's look at the steps involved that allows people to get control of their lives by mastering their workflow.

The idea expanded – key findings

'Stuff'

Whatever your role, 'stuff' comes in. By 'stuff', Allen means things about which we have some interest, concern, attention etc. but which needs clarification about our commitment to it and tracking of it.

'Stuff' needs to be transformed. Before it can be transformed it needs to be collected. We need to make sure that everything is collected somewhere *other than in our heads*. In other words we need a system we can trust and rely on which is not dependent on our memories.

Collection Devices

The collection tool is the *in-basket*. The in-basket is a tool for capturing both self-generated input and information coming from the outside. The in-basket may be a physical in-basket, a paper-based device, an electronic note-taking device, a voice0recording device or e-mail or other higher-tech device.

Most people do have in-baskets of sorts. But for an in-basket to work – whichever version is used – it has to meet three requirements:

- Every open loop must be in the collection system and out of your head.
- There must be as few collection devices as possible but as many as you need.
- They must be emptied regularly (this does not mean that you have to finish what's in the in-basket – just that you have to take it out, decide what it is and what should be done with it – i.e. you never put it back in!)

These collection tools should become part of one's everyday life-style constantly by one's side and easily and immediately accessible.

Emptying the Collection Device

The basic principle is that you cannot organise what is incoming –

you can only collect it and process it. You organise the actions you will need to take based on the decisions you have made about what needs to be done.

The very first question to ask about each item in the basket is 'what is it?' Or to be more precise, is it *actionable*?

If 'no' there are three options says Allen: *trash it, incubate it* (i.e. action may be needed later) or *reference it* (i.e. potentially useful later). **Each of these three categories needs to be effectively managed** and the book gives plenty of ideas and help.

If 'yes' (i.e. something needs to be done) two things need to be determined: what project or outcome does it belong to and to which you have committed? What is the next action required?

If it's about a project then it needs to be captured on a project list (Allen defines a project as any desired result that requires more than one action step – you don't 'do' a project, only the actions related to it usually through well-constructed milestones). A weekly review of the list will keep the item in mind.

If it's not related to a project, then it is an actionable item to be organised. By actionable, Allen means **the next physical, visible activity that needs to be engaged in order to move current reality toward completion.** So *next actions* that meet this criterion may come from the project list or straight out of the in-basket.

Once you have decided on the next action, there is a choice to be made: *Do it* (if it will take less than two minutes), *delegate it* (either to yourself at a future time or to someone else more appropriate) or *defer it* (for you to do later which will be tracked via Next Actions List). Think of these as the Three-Ds!

Next Action Categories

If you delegate an item then a *waiting-for* device will need to be set up to track progress. If you defer an item, then either it will need to be *calendarised* (specific time on a specific day) or it will go onto the *next actions list*. All actions therefore have one of three homes – the waiting-for device, the calendar or the next actions list.

This means **no more daily to-do lists**. All time-specific actions, day-specific actions and day-specific information are on the calendar. All other next actions are on the *next action list*. This list, together with the calendar, is at the heart of daily action-management organisation.

Sometimes, for very busy people (and recall John Egan – the original Chairman of Jaguar – who famously said 'business doesn't need busy fools'), the next actions list will need to be categorised. And Allen has a neat way of doing this. By convenience. Try categorising your next actions list by *phone, computer, shopping, office, etc.* So, as you find yourself in different locations (for example, near a computer, with time to use the mobile etc.) then take out the list and take an action.

Summary

By using a system that you can trust and rely on personal effectiveness increases. But the critical success factor is probably the weekly review. The weekly review is the time to gather and process all your stuff, review your system, update your lists and get clean, clear, current and complete. The more complete the system is and the more it is used the more it will be trusted. The more it is trusted the more complete you will be motivated to keep it. The weekly review is the master key to maintaining that standard.

The idea in practice – putting the idea to work

The practical implications? What one thing can I implement as a result of this research?

1. On one sheet of paper – preferably in diagrammatic form – describe the system you currently use to manage your workflow.

2. On a scale of 1-10 (1=Low Effectiveness/10=High Effectiveness) how effective do you rate your present system?

3. On another sheet of paper put in diagrammatic form the approach described in this article. Is it better than the one you are using? If yes, experiment with it for three months and then review.

READING 34

Business Behaving Badly

CHA

'Manners maketh man' – the title of a school essay once written by the author could usefully be re-titled 'manners maketh man *and business*' if the findings of a recent survey by the public relations firm CHA * are to be believed. Bad manners, apparently, are costing British business dear.

The research was conducted by Explorandum (an independent market research company, on behalf of CHA) in March 2006 using an online survey of 1103 employees in organisations with more than 10 staff. Telephone interviews with HR or communications professionals representing big employers were carried out to explore and record examples of best practice.

Reading 34 summarises the key findings of this research and highlights 'top tips' for engaging in, what the report refers to as 'corporate courtesy'. As the Financial Times commented (14 May 2006) the report provides 'a lesson both in man management – and manners'.

The idea in brief – the 'core' idea

The survey highlights how there has been a decline in all areas of business etiquette: being late for meetings, not paying suppliers on time, bosses dressing down subordinates in public, calls not being answered and customers being rude and even lying.

Then there are the peculiarly technological faux-pas – sharing email addresses with strangers, sending emails in place of telephone calls or meetings and castigating another person by email rather than face-to-face.

The perceived slow erosion of common courtesy appears to be gathering momentum and in response the Government has made 'respect' a key theme for its third term in office. This new survey suggests that courtesy also needs to find its way back into the workplace.

The idea expanded – key findings

1 The customer is king

Let's start with the good news. Customers are generally treated well. Over 80% of respondents said they always kept their promises to customers no matter what the obstacles were. However, the balance seems to have been tipped in that increasingly employees find themselves on the receiving end of badly behaved customers who use bullying tactics, engage in threatening behaviour or simply lie to get what they feel is theirs by right.

2 Visitors get treated well

Most companies now understand the impact of first impressions. Receptions tend to be well staffed, guests tend to be greeted appropriately and callers' first contact is positive:

- 75% of respondents say their switchboard responses are warm and friendly.
- 80% report that calls are almost always answered within four rings.
- 80% also say visitors are greeted warmly (although 40% claim they are kept waiting beyond their appointment time).

3 Leaders and managers get a mixed report

It's *inside* the organisation that the problems start. 30% of workers agree that phone calls tend to be treated as an interruption to real work. 60% say their organisation is slow to return calls. A third suggest people can be difficult to get hold of and hide behind their voicemail.

Employees report that where people feel they are in a stronger position rudeness is more likely to creep in:

- Over one third of employees say their boss praises them if they have done a good job or thanks the team for its efforts.
- Four out of 10 employees feel their organisations do not know how to give criticism constructively.
- Authority is often linked to abuse with nearly half of respondents saying they are sometimes bullied into doing things.
- Over four out of 10 employees report junior people are ignored in meetings.
- Public reprimand is a recurring theme with over half of respondents admitting they resort to reprimanding staff in front of others.

4 Mushroom management has not disappeared

While the will to keep people well informed appears to have increased (up from 44% to 65%) there is room for improvement in the methods used:

- Three in 10 still report that their organisation communicates big issues fairly badly or, at least, 'not very well'.
- Six out of 10 complain that communication is overcomplicated. *(Ed: see Harvard Business Review May 2006: The five messages leaders must manage).*
- Seven out of 10 respondents say they learn about changes that affect them later than they would like.
- A similar number continue to rely on the rumour mill to learn about their organisation's plans.

5 Employees have a love-hate relationship with email

Over-use of email can be a sign of laziness or used to avoid difficult conversations:

- Over half of respondents have seen email used when a meeting would have been appropriate.

211

- Nearly half say 'all addressee' emails are sent without proper thought adding to information overload and time wasting (for 20% this is a frequent occurrence).
- One in five employees say emails are used to reprimand or criticise staff.
- Half of respondents report that critical emails are copied to others in the organisation.

6 Poor meeting behaviour

The study revealed clear evidence of frustration about how people behave in meetings. The top complaints were:

- People try to dominate.
- Meetings over-run without checking with everyone it's OK.
- People turn up late.
- Meetings get cancelled at the last minute.
- People interrupt colleagues.
- Junior people get ignored.
- People constantly check emails or mobiles in meetings.

Although the survey did not investigate levels of rudeness per se the researchers were surprised at how often respondents commented on the amount of pure unpleasantness there can be in the office.

So what is the answer? What are the 'hot tips' for bringing common courtesy back into the workplace?

* Published with permission from CHA

The idea in practice – putting the idea to work

The practical implications? What one thing can I implement as a result of this research?

Ps and Qs

- Simply remember to say 'thank-you'.
- Treat others as you'd want to be treated (avoid aggression and rudeness).

- Actively listen – look at situations from both sides ('walk a mile in the other person's moccasins').
- Give others the benefit of the doubt.

Responding to phone calls

- Build in time for preliminaries at the start and end of the conversation.
- In an informal conversation gauge if it's appropriate to take a call rather than leave it to voicemail.
- Check your voicemail regularly – always respond within 24 hours.
- When on the phone focus on the conversation – people can hear key boards being tapped!

Dealing with third parties

- Greet visitors personally – don't send your 'underling'.
- Never keep visitors waiting beyond the appointed time without very good reasons that are explainable.
- Offer refreshments at meetings – easily overlooked.

Regard praise as a gift

- Praise people in a way that is meaningful to them (never stereotype corporate practice for the sake of it – e.g. hand written cards because 'that's the way the boss does it').
- Just say 'thank-you' face-to-face.

Email etiquette

- Before you hit the keyboard ask: 'is this really the most appropriate way to communicate?'
- Never, never use email to communicate a difficult message.
- Don't share email addresses with strangers.
- Check email regularly and (however hard) respond within 24 hours (maximum).

Manage meetings

- Circulate the agenda at least 24 hours in advance (ask for additional items).
- If you really can't attend alert people promptly and say why.
- Always start (even if everyone is not there) and finish on time (don't wait for stragglers and don't be one).
- Assign a note taker, circulate and file agreed actions, copy non-attendees.
- Give everyone the opportunity to contribute (*Ed: but don't seek consensus*).
- Be ruthless about blackberries and mobiles being switched off.

Dealing with difficult conversations

- Allow enough – but not too much – time.
- Meet face-to-face in private.
- Switch off your mobile (not to silent or vibrate).
- Build rapport – establish some common ground.
- Clearly state the purpose.
- Use collaborative language (shared problem solving).

Involve the team

- Communicate simply, frequently and clearly.
- Keep people informed from the start – not when it's too late.
- Tailor your communication – no 'wads' of information.
- Avoid jargon like the plague – speak plainly.
- Give time to digest information – seek feedback.

In the post-Enron era there has been an understandable tendency to bring corporate ethics back onto centre-stage – with the associated result of over-regulating what w as not regulated before. While this has helped to guard again corporate excess it has also had the effect of raising costs and dampening creativity at a time when innovation in business is badly needed.

Reintroducing common courtesy is a cost-effective way of ensuring that people's behaviour meets basic ethical standards. Bad manners come at a real cost to business.

For information about CHA go to www.chapr.co.uk where the complete report can be downloaded.

7

Postscript

READING 35

The Best of Peter Drucker

Dr Fred Cannon

For many of us in the management guru business there has always been only one guru: Peter Drucker who died at the end of 2005 at the age of 95 leaving behind a remarkable body of work, spanning 50 years, that not only addressed the major themes in modern management thinking but often anticipated them by decades.

But of course he was not a guru. He did not do 'fads'. He was a distinguished thinker who found his forte in the leadership of ideas rather than in the leadership of people and business – testimony to his own belief that success comes from concentrating on your strengths and putting yourself where your strengths can produce the best results and the most satisfaction (i.e. success).

This **Reading** is dedicated to his outstanding achievements. Without apology it is longer than most of the other readings in the book.

The idea in brief – the 'core' idea

For someone who produced 30 books over seven decades and even had another title in the pipeline at the time of his death makes it extraordinarily difficult to single out one 'core' idea. But weaving through his contributions that ranged from marketing to organisation was a central theme of **'what constitutes an effective executive?'**

Following on from his seminal *The Practice of Management* (1954) a number of his widely acclaimed articles focused on managing personal, people and business effectiveness reflecting a deeply held belief that management was essentially a social function that (by definition) attracted and required sociable people who could communicate and build effective relationships.

One of Drucker's more controversial views (at the time) was that an effective executive does not have be a leader in the sense that the term was commonly used. There were no templates and certainly no stereotypes. Says Drucker:

"The CEOs I worked with over 65 years were all over the map in terms of their personalities, attitudes, values, strengths and weaknesses. They ranged from extroverted to nearly reclusive, from easygoing to controlling, from generous to parsimonious. What made them effective is that they followed the same fundamental practices."

In this **Reading** we outline these fundamental practices and provide the nuggets that were quintessentially Drucker.

The idea expanded – key findings

Practice Number 1: Effective executives know how to manage themselves.

All great achievers have always managed themselves. Drucker framed seven straightforward questions that executives need to be able to answer to be effective:

Q1 What are my strengths? Concentrate on your strengths and put yourself where they can produce outstanding results.

To stay mentally alert and engaged during one's working life, one must know how and when to change the work one does.

Q2 How do I perform best? Like one's strengths how one performs is unique. Just as people achieve by doing what they are good at, they also achieve by working in ways that they perform best.

It takes far more energy to improve from incompetence to mediocrity than to improve from first-rate performance to excellence.

Q3 What are my values? Ask yourself: what kind of person do I want to see in the mirror in the morning? A person's strengths and the way that person performs rarely conflict. What one does well and successfully may or may not fit with one's value system. The work may not be worth devoting one's life to.

Q4 Where do I belong? Or rather, where do you not belong? The consultant who has learned that s/he does not perform well in large, bureaucratic firms should have learned to say no to joining one notwithstanding the status and rewards. Knowing where one belongs can transform a hard-working and competent person into an outstanding performer.

Q5 What should I contribute? What does the business situation require? Where and how can I achieve results that will make a difference within the next 12-18 months? They must be hard to deliver, within reach and meaningful. They should also be visible and measurable.

Q6 What are the strengths, the performance modes and values of my colleagues? Managing yourself requires taking responsibility for relationships – other human beings. You therefore have to be able to answer the same questions for the people you relate to on a daily basis.

Q7 How will you spend the second half of your life? Managing oneself increasingly leads you to begin to plan the second half of your life. And the one prerequisite for managing the second half is to begin doing so long before you enter it. Otherwise there is unlikely to be a second half – or one that you would not choose.

Practice Number 2: Effective executives know what needs to be done.

Note not 'what do you want to do' but 'what has to be done now'. Asking what has to be done, and taking the question seriously, is crucial for executive success. Failure to answer this question will render even the most able executive ineffectual.

Only when this question is answered does the next question feature: which of the two or three critical tasks am I best suited to undertake rather than delegate. Effective executives according to Drucker focus on jobs they will do especially well. They know that enterprises perform if top management performs – and don't if it doesn't.

Practice Number 3: Effective executives know what is right for the business.

Effective executives do not ask: is this right for the owners, the share price, the employees or the managers. While each stakeholder is important they know that a decision that isn't right for the business will ultimately not be right for any of the stakeholders.

Asking 'what is right for the business' does not guarantee that the right decision will be made. But failure to ask the question virtually guarantees the wrong decision.

Practice Number 4: Effective executives develop action plans.

Executives are doers. They execute. Effective executives define desired results by asking 'what contributions should the business expect from them over the next 18 months to two years?' What results will they commit to? With what deadlines? What are the constraints which if violated is certain to make the action both wrong and ineffectual?

The action plan is a statement of intentions rather than a commitment. There is a need to remain flexible as business conditions change. High level milestones rather than detailed actions allow this degree of flexibility.

219

The action plan will determine how the executive spends his or her time. Organisations are inherent time wasters. How the executive spends his or her time signals to the corporation what are priorities and what are not. If little or no time is spent on people matters then people will not be seen to matter. Actions speak louder than words.

Napoleon said no successful battle ever followed its plan. Kotter, a Harvard professor, remarked that you can't mange people into battle, you have to lead them. But without an action plan the executive becomes a prisoner of events. And without check-ins there is no way of knowing which events really matter and which are organisational noise. Clear direction backed up with well, thought through action plans combines leadership with management.

Practice Number 5: Effective executives make effective decisions.

Effective executives do not make a great many decisions. They focus on what is the most important. They try to make the few important decisions on the highest level of conceptual understanding.

Effective executives know when a decision has to be made on principle and when it should be made on the merits of the case. They know the difference between a compromise that is right and one that is wrong. They know that the most time consuming step is not making the decision but implementing it. They know that unless a decision has degenerated into work it is not a decision – it is at best a good intention.

Drucker was strong on being systematic in management. Characteristically, he outlined six steps in the decision-making process:

- *Classify the problem* – is it generic, exceptional or unique? The wrong decision will be made if the situation is classified incorrectly.

- *Define the real problem not the symptoms* – what exactly are we dealing with? There is only one safeguard against becoming a prisoner of an incomplete definition: check it again and again against all the observable facts and throw out a definition the moment it fails to encompass any of them.

- *Specify the answer to the real problem* – what are the 'boundary conditions' – the objectives the decision has to reach, the minimum goals it has to attain, the conditions it must satisfy. The most common cause of failure in a decision lies not in its being wrong initially. Rather, it is a subsequent shift in the goals – the specifications – which makes the prior right decision inappropriate.

- *Decide what is right rather than what is acceptable.* What will fully satisfy the specification before attention is given to the compromises, adaptations and concessions needed to make the decision acceptable. You can't make the right compromise unless you first know what right is.

- *Convert the decision into action.* No decision has been made unless carrying it out in specific steps has become someone's work assignment and responsibility. Until then it is merely an intention. An action is something someone can write into his or her schedules.

- *Test the decision.* Even the best decision has a high probability of being wrong. And the only way to test whether the assumptions on which the decision has been made are still valid is to go and look rather than to rely on abstract communications. Failing to go and look is the typical reason for persisting in a course of action long after it has ceased to be appropriate.

Making the important decision according to Drucker is the *specific executive task*. An effective executive makes these decisions as a systematic process with clearly defined elements and in a distinct series of steps.

Practice Number 6: Effective executives take responsibility for communicating the decision.

A decision is not final until people know:

- The name of the person accountable for carrying it out.
- The deadline.
- The names of the people who will be affected by the decision and therefore have to know about, understand and approve it.
- The names of the people who have to be informed of the decision even if they are not directly affected by it.
- What information they will need to get the job done.

Practice Number 7: Effective executives focus on opportunities rather than problems.

Problem solving does not produce results. It prevents damage. Exploiting opportunities produces results. Effective executives treat change as an opportunity rather than as a threat and assign their best people to opportunities not problems.

In areas where they are simply incompetent, smart executives don't make decisions or take actions. They delegate. Everyone has such areas.

Innovation is the orchestrated effort to create purposeful, focused change. Most successful innovations result from a conscious, purposeful search for opportunities. Drucker lists specific situations where such opportunities might be found:

- *Unexpected occurrences* in one's own company, a competitor or the industry (think post-its).

- *Exploiting incongruities* – gaps between what is and what could be in a market, a product or a process (think match boxes).

- *Changes in industry or market structure* – often those that change at great speed. New opportunities rarely fit the way the industry has always approached the market, defined it, or organised to serve it (think Dell). Traditional industry leaders repeatedly neglect the fastest growing segments (think Skype).

222

- *Demographic changes.* Innovation opportunities made possible by changes in demographics – whether numbers or characteristics – are among the most rewarding and least risky of entrepreneurial pursuits (think Saga).

- *Changes in perception.* Changing a manager's perception of a glass from half full to half empty opens up big innovation opportunities (think health: rather than rejoicing in great improvements in health most people still live in a state of collective hypochondria. The glass is clearly half-empty).

- *New knowledge or a new technology* – the superstars of innovation (think hovercraft, IPODs or wind farms).

Purposeful, systematic (that word again) innovation begins with the analysis of the sources of opportunities. It is both conceptual and perceptual. Successful innovators use both sides of their brains. To be effective an innovation has to be simple and it has to be focused. It should do only one thing. It should provoke the accolade 'but it's obvious!' Above all else innovation is hard, focused, purposeful work rather than genius. According to Drucker, entrepreneurship is the practice of systematic innovation.

Practice Number 8: Effective executives make meetings productive.

The key to running an effective meeting says Drucker is to decide in advance what kind of meeting it will be. Different kinds of meetings require different forms of preparation and different results. Making a meeting productive is largely a question of self-discipline. Decide what kind of meeting is needed, agree the format, stick to it and then sum up and close the meeting.

Drucker cites Alfred Sloan, the most effective business executive he ever knew:

"At the beginning of the meeting he announced the purpose. He then listened. He never took notes. He rarely spoke except to clarify a point. At the end he summed up, thanked the participants and left. Then he immediately wrote a short memo to one attendee spelling out the work assignment, setting the deadline and confirming the executive who would be accountable. He sent a copy to all attendees. Through such effective follow-up he made himself into an outstandingly effective executive."

Practice Number 9: Effective executives think and say 'we' rather than 'I'.

Effective executives know that they have ultimate responsibility, which can be neither shared nor delegated. But they know they have authority only because they have the trust of the organisation or team. This means they think of the organisation's needs ahead of their own. 'We' not 'I' reflects this belief. (Note the similarity decades later with the concept of humility in 'From Good to Great'.).

Practice Number 10: Effective executives understand the theory of their business.

Probably the most important practice of all.

Whenever a large organisation gets into trouble – especially if it's been successful – people understandably blame arrogance, complacency, bureaucracy or 'the culture'.

Rarely the case says Drucker. The root cause of nearly every such crisis is that *the assumptions* on which the organisation has been built no longer fit reality (think General Motors, IBM, Marks & Spencer). These assumptions are what Drucker meant by a company's *theory of business* (later translated into more exotic terminology by gurus with a less rigorous approach).

Drucker's theory of the business had three parts:

- Assumptions about the *business environment* – what an organisation gets paid for.
- Assumptions about the *business mission* – what an organisation considers as meaningful results.
- Assumptions about the *core competencies* – what an organisation must excel at to maintain leadership.

It gets better!

Four golden rules make a theory of business valid:

1. The assumptions must fit reality.
2. The assumptions in all three areas must fit one another.
3. The theory of the business must be known, understood and shared.
4. The assumptions must be tested constantly.

As Drucker articulated, some theories of business are so powerful that they last for a very long time. But eventually every one becomes obsolete. *(Ed: even Tesco!)*

Miracle workers – leaders on white horses – are sought to turn ailing organisations around (think M&S again). Those that manage it successfully tend to change the theory of their business (think Sony). They accept that a theory's obsolescence is a degenerative disease that will not be cured by procrastination but by decisive executive action.

Bonus Practice: Listen first, speak last.

Or to quote Covey (decades later): 'seek first to understand then be understood'.

Effectiveness is a discipline. Like every discipline it can be learned. But it must also be earned.

Drucker's most lasting thought:

"There is only one valid definition of a business purpose: to create a customer. Markets are not created by God, nature or economic forces, but by businessmen."

As the *Financial Times* so rightly commented, this is what Tesco has done so well – putting customers at the heart of what it does. It's a discipline. It's what Drucker was preaching 20 years ago.

The idea in practice – putting the idea to work

The practical implications? What one thing can I implement as a result of this research?

Are you a good fit with your organisation?

Take a pen and blank sheet of paper. Draw three circles. Label each My Strengths, My Values, My Organisation.

Ask: to what extent do these three circles overlap – i.e. how good is the fit between your strengths (talent) and your values (passion)? How good is the fit between your strengths (talent) and the organisation for which you work? How good is the fit between your values (passion) and the organisation for which you work?

The bigger the overlap the better the fit. Where is the overlap smallest (or not at all)? What are the implications? What executive actions will you take to resolve this?

Now take your strengths (talent) circle. Underneath list the three most important tasks you are currently engaged on. How good is the fit between your strengths (talent) and your critical tasks?

If poor, what tasks would represent a better fit? What executive actions will you take to focus on these rather than your existing tasks?

Are you opportunity or problem focused?

Now take two more blank sheets of paper. On the first write down a short list of the most significant opportunities facing your business (team, unit or activity). On the second sheet write a list of the very best people you have.

To what extent are your best people engaged on your most significant opportunities? If not, what executive actions will you take to re-deploy them?

(For a management team get each member to compile the two lists. Then use a team meeting to distil the lists into two master lists to match the best people with the best opportunities. Revise this every six months).

Does your theory of business hold water?

Your final sheet of paper.

Can you write down the fundamental assumptions that underlie your business model? Try it. Talk to a few colleagues to see if they agree. If you are not in a part of the business where this is obvious make an effort to talk to someone who is. Your future livelihood may depend on it!

Now comes the difficult part. What is the evidence (the facts) that these assumptions are valid – i.e. fit with current reality? (For example, what would a representative sample of non-customers say if you tested the assumptions on them?).

If the evidence is lacking – or weak – what executive action will you take to influence the situation? When will you take it? Who else might be involved?

Drucker's final words of wisdom

"Management is doing things right; leadership is doing the right things."

"What motivates knowledge workers is what motivates volunteers...they need, above all, challenges."

"The one person to distrust is the one who never makes a mistake...either s/he is phoney, or stays with the tried and trivial. The better a person is, the more mistakes s/he will make."

"Plans are only good intentions unless they immediately degenerate into hard work."

"A poor organisation structure makes good performance impossible, no matter how good the individual managers may be."

"It can be said there are no underdeveloped countries (Ed: insert people). There are only under-managed ones."

8

Reflective Summary

OED, my consulting practice, has been in business for 10 years. This book was written partly to celebrate that fact. Add to that 10 years another decade as a practising consultant and the same again as a practising manager then it's fair to say that 'I've been around for a time.'

During this time, 'much has changed and 'little has changed'. In the 'much' category I would put technology and globalisation as the most significant forces for change. When I first became a HR Manager with Ford, Europe was a brand new concept and the organisation was essentially a collection of national entities. There were no PCs and main frame computers were limited to payroll and other complex administrative tasks. The twin forces of technology and globalisation have transformed the way businesses are structured and the way they are managed. So much is clear.

But it is in the 'little' category where the surprises and disappointments lie. When I decided to go to business school to do an MBA I sincerely believed that I would learn tools and approaches that would help address the big issues of the day. Not least among these were the challenges of understanding employee behaviour and figuring out how to manage ('leading' people had not yet entered the regular business vocabulary), motivate and reward people based on different assumptions than in the past. My own professor, the late Tom Lupton, was an inspiration in this respect.

Research spurned and papers were published, largely driven by the individual interests of professors and their research staff, the output of which formed a good part of the MBA curriculum.

Unsurprisingly, the debate started about the usefulness or otherwise of business schools and the ever-increasing number of MBAs entering largely the blue chip investment banks and the top consulting firms. I was genuinely shocked when a fellow classmate admitted to me that during his two years at business school he had not learnt one thing that he could directly apply in the real world he was about to enter.

In spite of the proliferation of business schools across the world and widely popularised contributions from the new breed of management gurus, we still have no truly coherent theory of business (notwithstanding Drucker's huge contribution), no enduring principles of leadership and no co-ordinated body of research designed to move the practice of management into a different league. How is it that after 30 years' in management, consulting and academe, I continue to see articles being published addressing questions that were being asked at the start of my career? If we don't know 'how to motivate people' (or 'talent' as it is now fashionably called) by now, I suggest that we never will. Can we really put our hands on our hearts and say that we have had a good return on our investment? Look around you. What, if anything do you see that is radically different? Somewhat less command and control, maybe. A bit more emphasis on innovation, perhaps. More lip service given to teamwork, certainly. But the developments that have occurred have been incremental, piece-meal and ad hoc rather than unifying, coherent and transforming. Even leadership, with its phenomenal output in recent years, remains a black art.

Many argue that management is, or should be, a profession (where would that leave leadership?). But can we really say that management is a profession in the same way that medicine or law or even engineering is? Have the advances in management – such as they have been – been as fundamental and long lasting as the advances in medicine? What is the managerial equivalent to discovering penicillin in the business world? How does our academic training (any old first degree plus an MBA from schools with widely differing reputations) compare with medical or legal training? Why haven't the medical schools diversified in the same way as business

229

schools? What is the business equivalent of the time trainee doctors spend on hospital placement? Do you trust and respect your boss as much as you trust and respect your GP or consultant? Would you let your CEO fly a jumbo jet? Sit side-by-side a leading medical journal with a leading business journal. Look at the statistical and intellectual rigour. How do they compare? We fall short of any scientific ideal. No wonder the Harvard Business Review is known in some academic circles as the Heathrow Press!

But in management, science doesn't matter of course. Push evidence aside and focus on the soft, immeasurable skills that capture the attention of reality-based managers. Bleat on about the need for vision, mission and values but truly great companies do very special things and are led by CEOs who are largely unknown to the population at large. Who knows who the CEOs are of Esso, Mercedes and JP Morgan, for example? But successful companies do not require reality-based leaders to lead them. They need CEOs who thoroughly understand the industry in which they operate, who have credibility and respect in their own organisations and have the courage, character and conviction to 'do things their way'.

I do not profess to know the answers to the questions I raise but I know that the questions need to be asked. I also know that managers need to manage and leaders need to lead based on more than book jacket blurbs however convincing. Drucker attempted to formulate a theory of business. Most of us have forgotten where theory comes from because of our obsession with quick action. A theory is based on thorough observation and description of phenomenon. These phenomenon are then carefully categorised so that researchers can highlight their most meaningful differences. Then hypotheses can be developed of what causes the phenomenon to happen and why. Then you have a theory from which to make predictions and through an iterative process end up with something that explains across a wide range of circumstances. Business schools need to ensure that every MBA student ingrains this way of thinking into their management psyche. It was John Maynard Keynes who said that practical men ...are usually the slaves of some defunct economist. For 'economist' insert 'theory'. Management thinkers seem to have lost sight of this important point.

9

Home Truths

10 Lessons from Experience

1. **See the big picture.** Continually apply the 'Drucker Test' – do the assumptions on which the business has been built still fit reality? What are the trends? Root down to determine whether they confirm the latter or suggest something else. What is really happening out there? Remember, even John Thain, ex- CEO of Merryl Lynch and widely recognised as a world-class analyst – failed to see the 2008 credit crunch coming with consequences for the firm and for him.

2. **Be crystal clear about the direction, focus and priorities of the business.** Ensure these are collectively owned and the executive team is held accountable for them. Articulate them. Repeat the core message. Symbolise it. Link promotion and rewards to those who genuinely reflect what matters to the business as a whole.

3. **Lead from both the front and the back.** People need clarity about where they are going but they also need encouragement. Get too far ahead and you will leave people behind. They won't be there when you look behind. Help them to keep up. Reward the acquisition of new skills as much as you reward. Be ready to catch people when they fall.

4. **Always focus on performance.** As Jack Welch, former CEO of General Electrics, was fond of reminding us, developing your

career is secondary to performance. Do everything with a sense of urgency and drive to win. Make a difference on every job. Develop a reputation for exceeding people's expectations. But do it in a way that people value and respect.

5.   **Don't go with the herd.** Look at things in different ways. Bring people in who can offer a different point of view. See the organisation as a hierarchy of ideas rather than a hierarchy of experience. Think the unthinkable. Discuss the undiscussable. Be provocative. Be different. Do things your way.

6.   **Keep things simple.** 'As simple as you can – as complex as you must.' Avoid clutter. Avoid layers. Avoid HR-speak. Encourage directness, openness and candour. Again, remember Jack Welch's words: we gave chosen one of the world's more simple professions.

7.   **Don't let business take over your life – or anyone else's.** Business is there to support life not the other way round. Be clear about the three most important things in your life. Do not let your work life destroy these. Make sure everyone understands this. 24/7 work-styles are – or should be – a thing of the past. Who you are is more important than what you have. Work on it!

8.   **Ignore the management gurus.** Do not be led astray. With the possible exception of Drucker, there is no management book equivalent to Keynes General Theory of Employment or Adam Smith's Wealth of the Nations. Wrap you business around the customer not the latest fad.

9.   **Stick to your principles.** Have the courage to resign. Your reputation and your legacy are more important than short-term gain. Always do what you believe to be right. But know what these very few, basic principles are and let others know what they are in the way that you act. There is only one person you see in the mirror – you need to like what you see.

10. **Finally, remember Drucker's words:** "There is only one valid definition of a business purpose: to create a customer. Markets are not created by God, nature or economic forces, but by businessmen."

Tools

Appendix I

Effective Organizational Leadership (EOL)

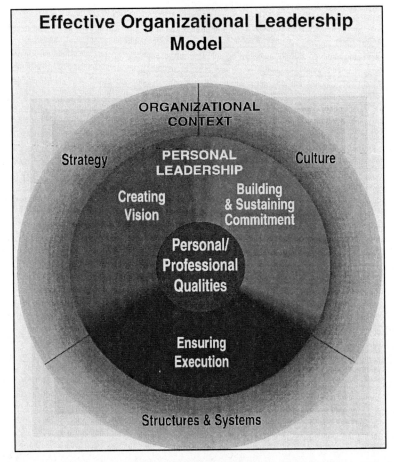

Effective Organizational Leadership Model

ORGANIZATIONAL CONTEXT

Strategy

Culture

PERSONAL LEADERSHIP

Creating Vision

Building & Sustaining Commitment

Personal/ Professional Qualities

Ensuring Execution

Structures & Systems

© Harbridge House Inc. 1993 (Pricewaterhouse Coopers). Modified from original research by OED Consulting Ltd. 2003 and used with permission.

The inner ring (PPQ) and the three segments (Creating Vision, Building & Sustaining Commitment and Ensuring Execution) were described in Chapter 2. Essentially, these represent the clusters of 42 leader behaviours that are tabulated in Appendix II and have been shown to have high internal consistency and reliability as measured by Cronbach Alphas (Range 0.77-0.90).

These behaviours do not happen in a vacuum. A leader's personal vision is shaped – and might indeed shape – the broader vision and *strategy* of the organisation as a whole. A leader's ability to build and sustain commitment will be shaped – and might also shape – the wider organisation's values and *culture*. A leader's ability to execute will be shaped – and might also shape – the broader *structures and systems* of the organisation. For truly effective organisational leadership to exist there will need to be full alignment across the model.

The job of senior management is to make effective decisions in each of the three segments of the outer ring. It is therefore the senior management that will set the context for the behaviours that individual leaders practise. In turn, these decisions will reflect senior management's response to the degree of turbulence in the external business environment including competitor activity. Organisational leaders manage the interface between the organisation and its environment where the fulcrum for significant change resides.

When organisations get 'out of skew' behaviours follow. For example, in the early days of Apple Computer under Steve Jobs vision was very high, as was commitment. Execution left a lot to be desired. It was an exciting place to work, inspiring but its management was weak leading to significant leadership changes and deteriorating commercial performance. When Jobs was replaced the company swung in the opposite direction – it followed strict management discipline but lost its vision as an innovative, inspirational company.

Another example is Ford. Always a well-managed company – tight, disciplined and focused – but somehow lacking a big vision complicated by the level of involvement by the Ford family. People performed well, put in huge efforts but did not display the kind of excitement and buzz generated in a company like Apple (or more recently, Google).

Commitment is the one managers tend to get away with. While a company may be low on vision or execution it is often still high on commitment. Put simply, senior managers are trading off the natural commitment most people bring to their jobs. But usually this effect is short term. Sooner or later a company that shows lack of direction or fails to get things done will lose the commitment of its people. It is a constant juggling act to balance vision, commitment and execution across an organisation at different times in changing circumstances. But it is the job of senior organisational leaders.

Take a few minutes to reflect on this very simple model and consider the following questions:

Q1 How would you rate your organisation (High, Medium, and Low) in terms of Vision, Commitment and Execution?

Q2 What does it feel like to work in an organisation with this profile? How would you like it to change? Why?

Q3 How is the profile related to each of the three outer ring segments? What might senior management do to influence behaviours more positively around a different profile?

Appendix II

Leader Behaviours

Work through each of the behaviours below assigning a score (1=Low; 5=High) that reflects your own effectiveness. Work out your averages for each segment and insert. Examine cluster scores (for example, *Defining Expectations* versus *Recognising Contributions*).

Then answer the questions at the end of the exercise.

Creates Vision ('Sets direction')	
Understands the External Environment 1. Understands and communicates the critical factors for success in the marketplace 2. Actively identifies and responds to clients' needs	
Understands the organisation 3. Understands the strengths and limitations of the organization 4. Knows how to work across organisational boundaries	
Defines Purpose and Inspires 5. Develops a sense of larger purpose or context to guide others' activities 6. Articulates the vision and direction so that others understand what is important	
Translates Purpose into Action 7. Clearly explains the purpose and relative priorities of initiatives, projects and tasks 8. Helps others to translate the vision and direction into specific objectives / action plans 9. Helps other anticipate and respond to change	
Average:	

Builds and Sustains Commitment ('Aligns people')	
Communicates 10. Encourages the open expression of ideas and opinions 11. Listens to – and considers – what others have to say 12. Engages others in discussion to develop a shared vision **Involves** 13. Helps others understand how they can contribute to the achievement of an initiative or project 14. Involves others in developing goals or objectives **Supports** 15. Ensures others have the resources needed to deliver results 16. Prevents distractive influences from interfering from getting the job done 17. Champions positions taken by others when s/he feels they are right **Influences** 18. Leverages informal contacts and networks to build support for getting things done 19. Provides one-to-one briefings on important issues and developments 20. Encourages cross-functional collaboration in generating ideas, suggestions and a range of solutions to problems **Promotes Team Work** 21. Conducts team meetings in a way that builds trust and mutual respect 22. Gives others the freedom they need to do their jobs 23. Leverages the knowledge and skills of colleagues and / or team members 24. Recognises collective as well as individual contributions	
Average:	

Ensures Execution ('Makes things happen')	
Manages Performance	
Defines Expectations	
25. Explains individual roles and responsibilities	
26. Delegates responsibility and authority appropriately	
27. Expects high performance from self and others	
Monitors Progress	
28. Follows-up with others on important issues and/or assignment	
29. Confronts performance issues, working with others to resolve them	
Recognises Contributions	
30. Uses recognition, praise and other methods to reward good performance	
31. Recognises others for good performance more often than criticises them for poor performance	
Builds Capability	
32. Provides others with a variety of assignments to develop new skills	
33. Encourages innovation and calculated risk taking in others	
34. Actively coaches others on how to learn from their experiences and improve themselves professionally	
35. Provides open and honest feedback	
Average:	

Personal & Professional Qualities ('You')	
36. Treats with others with respect	
37. Displays a strong sense of personal integrity	
38. Seeks and accepts personal responsibility and accountability	
39. Seeks opportunities for continuous improvement and profess-ional 'stretch' rather than continuing to do what is 'comfortable'	
40. Exhibits energy and enthusiasm in performing his / her job	
41. Continually seeks ways to improve current performance	
42. Changes own position when a convincing case is made	
Average:	

Q1 In terms of Vision, Commitment and Execution what is your profile? Where are you strong (4-5), moderate (3), weak (1-2)? What are the implications of this?

Q2 What are your:

- Five highest ratings?

- Five lowest ratings

- Top three 'clusters'

- Bottom three 'clusters'

What is this telling you? What, if anything, are the patterns telling you?

Q3 Distil the above into the three most important messages for you as a leader.

Appendix III

Performance Improvement Grid (PIG)

Using the data from Appendices I & II, and reflecting heavily on your own self-awareness and experience as a leader, identify those leader-related behaviours, which if actioned, will help improve your leadership effectiveness. Start with an active verb:

1. What should I *start* doing to help improve my effectiveness as a leader?

2. What should I *stop* doing to help improve my effectiveness as a leader?

3. What should I *continue doing/do more of* to help improve my effectiveness as a leader?

4. What is the single most important message I have for myself as a leader?

5. How might I check that I have been honest with myself, got things broadly right?